The New Creation Mother

Raising Godly Children **Preserving God's Heritage**

The New Creation Mother

Raising Godly Children   **Preserving God's Heritage**

by

Winifred Obinna

Raising Godly Children Preserving God's Heritage

Printed in the U.S.A. 2022

Cover design and interior layout design by Uberwriters Christian Ghostwriters
www.uberwriters.com

Author Photograph by Keva Burns Johannes
© CustoMYze Me Ltd. Co.

ISBN 979-8-9860177-0-9 Paperback
ISBN 979-8-9860177-1-6 eBook

This book is dedicated to:

Jesus, my Lord, my ALL!

My three children, Kingsley, Angel, and Christian who are my extraordinary gift and great reward.

My husband Kingsley Snr., for your dedication and commitment to partnering with me to raise godly children, and for all the support and encouragement in writing this book.

Contents

Introduction

In 2016 the Lord directed me to start the Mothers in Christ initiative, a prayer group located in Dallas, Texas. Our primary assignment is that of intercession. So after many hours of praying over many years, God began to clearly reveal the significant gaps most Christian mothers experience in their understanding and daily implementation of the Word of God. This first became evident to me when I saw a range of afflictions, expressed in various ways, that creep into homes and oppress families. Many times things can creep in without our permission, but they certainly need our permission to stay. Afflictions such as sickness, disabilities, and rebellion—to name a few. The worst part is, these afflictions are especially affecting our children in significantly damaging ways.

In writing this book, my vision is to encourage and equip Christian mothers to wholeheartedly commit to raising godly children and thereby preserve the next generation. If we fail, this world is in deep trouble. I envision this assignment being successfully completed through Christian mothers stepping into their office as priests over their children, their homes, and ultimately, over their world. The goal for each one of us is to exalt the Kingdom of God, and my hope is to be a stirring voice to Christian women in my generation. The goal is to wake women up, push them to recalibrate, encourage them in their fight of faith in these very serious end times, and hopefully to win unbelieving mothers to Christ through the compelling, Spirit-filled truths presented in this book.

Some Straight Talk

For this book to be of any use to you, you have to decide where you stand with God. You need to understand where you belong. This is a book for *Christian* mothers. We're talking to the Christian woman, charging her with what has now become a do-or-die mission. The reality of the matter is when women are born again, plenty of them are not taught who they truly are as a new creation in Jesus Christ, nor how to stand against the challenges coming against them on a daily basis. By the end of this book, that issue will be resolved.

Understand that the Christian mother has a critical and specific assignment when it comes to raising her children, and this ties in to who she is in Christ. Her first step is realizing she is only a steward of what she has been given, and that her children truly belong to God. The critical part is she must therefore raise her children according to God's plan and not *her* plan. She has to rely on the Holy Spirit for His specific direction intended for each child.

A key to success is remaining spiritually minded. As New Creation Mothers, our example is Jesus. *He* was spiritually minded during His time on Earth so *we* need to be spiritually minded. When Jesus walked the Earth He revealed and modeled the perfect connection between the spiritual world and the physical world. When He encountered someone who was sick, Jesus didn't advise them to take some herbs or tell them to lie down. He commanded deaf ears to be opened, He spoke healing to the lame, and He cast out evil spirits.

God is spirit (John 4:24) and God created us, therefore our origin is spiritual. Romans 8:5 tells us that to be carnally minded is death. To live and walk wisely we need to walk in the Spirit and to be spiritually minded. We have been born by the Spirit of God into the Spirit, so our entire consciousness should be spiritual. Understanding the spirituality of life is where the victory really is and where life's purpose resides. How do we walk in the Spirit? I'll go into much more detail in the coming pages but Bible study and daily prayer—specifically praying in the Spirit, which will be covered later— is the quick answer.

In contrast, our secular culture is actively (and often successfully) trying to lure our children away from God. This is done through negative portrayals of the Church and her spiritual values, as well as the temptation to partake in youthful lusts, activities, and attitudes. More than ever, Christian mothers need to diligently pray for their families, purposefully leading their children in biblical principles. With the plan for a demonic New World Order marching to a brazenly escalated timeline, the push to administer experimental but widely touted vaccines to our children, complex social issues like Critical Race Theory, transgender controversies, preschool sexual education, and so much more facing us, Christian mothers need Spirit-filled wisdom more than ever. We need to wake up from our secular slumber, we need to stay educated about what the current culture is exposing our children to, and we need the direction of the Holy Spirit to successfully navigate these dark waters. We simply can no longer put our trust in the system of this world. We have to put our trust in God.

We simply can no longer put our trust in the system of this world. We have to put our trust in God.

What You Will Gain

In this book, you will learn the immense power of becoming a New Creation Mother, and what it means for you as a career woman, or a stay-at-home mom. You will discover what it means for you as a wife. What it means as someone taking care of aging parents, or someone whose child is facing some health challenge, social challenge, academic challenge, or any challenge really. Using biblical examples, and some profound, illustrative examples from my personal experience, you will learn exactly how to apply these truths in a practical way with distinct and notable results.

There is a very serious call to action in this book. Now that the alarm has been sounded, and you, the New Creation Mother, are about to know and apply the truths revealed in *The New Creation Mother,* you will quickly realize you have an enemy in the wild and he does not fight fair. You not only have a responsibility to act, *you have a calling.* That you need to accept this call, and make the necessary changes in your life cannot be emphasized enough.

I would like to make it clear at this point that this is not a step-by-step, formulaic manual. The reason for this is we all have different callings, different environments, different challenges. What we have in common is we have been given authority on this Earth by God, and have been provided with a set of practical tools to carry out that authority.

We will go into this in more detail but for now, these tools include the Word of God and prayer. The first tool you have is actually a weapon—the sword of the Spirit. When you speak the Word of God (scripture) with your mouth, it is a weapon to powerfully inflict damage on evil, and carry out *The New Creation Mother's* affairs. Your *mouth* in submission to, and under the guidance of the Holy Spirit, is a potent weapon indeed. I chart the course of my life and calling with my mouth, by speaking the Word of God over it. This comes by prayer, but also from engaging the Holy Spirit within me to empower me, speaking the Word of God. Proverbs 18:21 tells us life and death are in the power of the tongue and this is entirely true. Your mouth carries the sword of the Spirit when you speak the Word of God with your God-given authority (Luke 10:19, Luke 19:13).

My intention in the following chapters is to make you aware of the authority you have, and to guide you in using these spiritual tools so you can apply them to your specific calling, environment, and challenges. Again, this takes a daily relationship with the Holy Spirit, but then you will begin to successfully live an abundant and victorious life as a New Creation Mother.

On the note of differing environments, something I've realized is that, compared to the early Church, the way we've been doing church is relatively new. We're learning a lot as we go, for example, the modern concept of church has typically been implemented as a one-size-fits-all model. When Jesus gave us the instruction to go into all the world and preach the gospel, for me as a mother He is telling me to go into *my* world—to preach the gospel in *my* sphere of influence, and to those mothers. For me as an author, I understand my specific calling is to go into my world of publishing and preach the gospel. In addition, my calling as a businesswoman is to spread the gospel in the business world.

We are called to be a voice ministering to the specific

needs of our individual worlds through the leading of the Holy Spirit. Let's say Elizabeth is a mother, and also the assistant soccer coach at her child's school, while being employed as a nurse. At a parent's meeting, she meets Winnie, her son's friend's mom, who shares the gospel with her from a mother's perspective. Then at soccer practice, Jennifer shares the gospel with her from a coaching and leadership viewpoint. Finally at the hospital she hears the gospel from the orderly, Mendez, in a healing and caregiving context. Elizabeth has now heard the gospel in three specific scenarios of her own life, from loving people she can relate to. How likely do you think it is that one of these seeds will land in some good ground of her heart, on the right day? Yes, I agree. It's very likely.

The key here is that because we wear multiple hats in our lifetime, we need to understand how to navigate these different aspects and environments. We don't put off our Christianity because we're doing mom stuff, or because we're at work. The takeaway here is, none of these roles operate in isolation.

In wrapping up this introduction, *The New Creation Mother* is for the Christian mother who is ready to start living a truly Christ-centered life, with truly supernatural results. It is intended to teach and encourage, and hopefully to be referred to when needed. As I mentioned earlier, there will be some examples and anecdotes in the book from my own life and experience. You will read about a woman who often didn't get it right the first time but resolved to not continue repeating her mistakes. Some mistakes are utterly heartbreaking and costly, and some may require greatly developed faith to "undo."

I had to pick a side to stand on and resolve to never be double-minded. The examples I use from my own life and experience are merely to illustrate specific points. They are not formulas, and they are certainly not to be treated as gospel—you need to find God's direction for your own life! The examples I use are from my own learning along the way and I will always quote the scripture reference for any point I make. Never take another person's experience as gospel, and always weigh any advice against scripture. It is crucial you apply the Word

It is crucial you apply the Word of God before acting on any advice you receive.

of God before acting on any advice you receive. Most people know they require change in their life, but often have no idea where to start, or how to go about making the changes they need. My hope is this book will be a power-tool for Christian mothers, an encouraging voice, a sounding board of truths that will remain with you for a lifetime, and a means of implementing consistent victory in your life.

I'm excited! Let's get started.

1

ARE YOU SAFE?

We live in a society where urgency frequently distracts from what is truly important, and deception is regularly presented as truth. It may not be overtly apparent to many people so I believe it is crucial to highlight the reality of the world our children are presently being raised in. In the consequent uncertainty created by this absence of clarity, we risk failing to recognize the most severe threats facing those we love. We are not, however, the first society to face this risk. In Amos 6:1-7 we read that around 760 BC God sent a message to the people in the northern kingdom of Israel through a shepherd named Amos. The message God sent to His people warned against complacency and passive indifference to the sin occurring all around them. This message, sent to alert the children of God, stands as true today as it did then.

Alert against Complacency

I'm sure you agree that our families are too precious to entrust their mental, physical, and spiritual health to any system, organization, or government, however well intentioned. This means it is up to us as mothers to be consciously and constantly seeking out the Holy Spirit's guidance in all things relating to our family's spiritual, mental, and physical wellbeing.

A biblical example we can draw from is found in the second chapter of the book of Joshua. When a Canaanite woman named Rahab heard the Israelite army was camped across the Jordan River she recognized the danger confronting Jericho, her home city. Instead of entrusting her family's lives to Jericho's leaders and their defense system, she actively sought a way to save them herself. Putting her own life at risk, she hid three Israelite spies on the roof of her house and bargained with them for her family's safety:

> "[12] Now therefore, I beg you, swear to me by the Lord, since I have shown you kindness, that you also will show kindness to my father's house, and give me a true token, [13] and spare my father, my mother, my brothers, my sisters, and all that they have, and deliver our lives from death." Joshua 2:12-13

As a prostitute, Rahab was fully aware of the wickedness that pervaded her city, and indeed all of Canaan. Her unwillingness to leave the welfare of her family in the hands of the society they lived in preempted her decisive action which would change the course of their future. Rahab's actions took foresight, planning, and courage, resulting in her family being the only people saved from the destruction that fell on the city:

> [23] And the young men who had been spies went in and brought out Rahab, her father, her mother, her brothers, and all that she had. So they brought out all her relatives and left them outside the camp of Israel. [24] But they burned the city and all that *was* in it with fire. Joshua 2:23-24

Rahab's insight into the threat her family faced, her proactive planning, and her bold move to change the situation are an excellent case study of how, today, we cannot sit idle as the world exerts its corrupt influence on our families.

Why Now?

One of the reasons for writing this book is to alert mothers to the reality that the family unit, and children especially, face a graver threat in these end times than ever before. Some examples of this are evident when considering how common divorce and single motherhood have become due to the covenant of marriage being disregarded, and even scorned in western society. Abortion is deemed "essential" to reducing the world's population growth[1], and the overall health of children has deteriorated at an alarming rate.

I would like to be crystal clear on this point because these threats have not arisen coincidentally—they are the result of an orchestrated spiritual attack on this generation. Paul explains this is in his letter to the Ephesians: "For we do not wrestle against flesh and blood, but against principalities, against powers, against the rulers of the darkness of this age, against spiritual hosts of wickedness in the heavenly places" (Ephesians 6:12).

I believe the enemy has increased his spiritual attack on this generation for various reasons. I think his main thrust is to discourage people from relying on God's Word within their daily lives, and to create doubt in every believer's faith-walk. The enemy's wiles have also led modern societies to rely more heavily on their governments, many of which are working closely with big tech, biotech/big pharma, and energy companies that are, sadly, mostly profit-driven, instead of bringing health, social unity, and wellbeing to our societies. To provide an idea of the level of attack the enemy has brought against this generation, a few statistics are listed below:

Physical[2] and Mental[3] Disorders in U.S. Children

- 54% percent of American children are chronically ill.

- 13% of America's children are in special education.

- One in six children has a developmental disorder.

- Millions suffer from allergies, including deadly peanut allergies.

- Almost 11% have attention deficit hyperactivity disorder (ADHD).

- 15,000 or more children were diagnosed with cancer in 2021 alone.

- One in 59 children has autism.

- ADHD, behavioral problems, anxiety, and depression are the most commonly diagnosed mental disorders in children.

- 9.4% of children aged 2-17 years (approximately 6.1 million) have received an ADHD diagnosis.

- 7.4% of children aged 3-17 years (approximately 4.5 million) have a diagnosed behavior problem.

- 7.1% of children aged 3-17 years (approximately 4.4 million) have been diagnosed with anxiety-related issues.

- 3.2% of children aged 3-17 years (approximately 1.9 million) have been diagnosed with clinical depression.

This enemy described in Ephesians 6 will use any avenue possible for evil, including national health and educational organizations, mainstream and social media, even governments—if any of the people in these organizations make themselves available to evil—to popularize and legitimize wicked tactics. In fact, in recent years the plan to reorder the world has been greatly accelerated, intentionally bringing chaos, shame, and confusion into young lives by the introduction of concepts like Critical Race Theory, and the introduction of homosexual and transgender "education" into even elementary schools.

An alarming insight into the plan became apparent when in 2021 the US Assistant Secretary for Health, a prominent transgendered politician, refused to answer the question asking whether all children should be allowed to select their gender and have access to government-funded sex reassignment surgery without parental notification or authorization[4].

Now, before we begin to despair, we may be living in a fallen world but as Christian mothers we are not of this world (John 15:19), and as such don't need to conform or submit to the traits and practices of the world. Recognizing these powers of darkness is not to be perceived in a spirit of fear but rather to serve as a revelation that we cannot fight this onslaught against our families without the guidance and assistance of God's Holy Spirit. We must not allow the global drive towards a new world order to dictate how we live. As New Creation Mothers we must establish our world inspired by the will of God and create the world we want to live in. In essence, we must bring Heaven down to Earth, as commanded by our Lord Jesus in Matthew 6:10.

As New Creation Mothers we must establish our world inspired by the will of God and create the world we want to live in.

This is only possible by understanding who we are in Christ and using the immensely powerful tools and weapons at our disposal, but I will cover more on this later.

Be Spiritually Minded

What does it mean to live *in* this world but not be *of* the world? When we choose to accept the redeeming sacrifice Jesus made for us on the cross and decide to live our life for Him we become a new person—we are spiritually born again, or born *(anew) from above*[5]. Once we've been born from above we no longer belong to this world but become citizens of Heaven (Philippians 3:20) living our life on Earth until the day we join our Savior, Jesus Christ, in Heaven. Consequently, even though we remain on Earth we live in two worlds. There is a natural world, and there is a spiritual world. We must be conscious of the spiritual world to which we belong.

Following Jesus means He is the example we must live by, and when Jesus walked the Earth He was at all times fully conscious of the spiritual realm. He knew His purpose on Earth and saw important spiritual connections where few others were able to perceive these connections. In order to see beyond the physical world like Jesus did, you need to be led by the Holy Spirit. When the religious leaders of the time heard how Jesus was teaching the people differently from how *they* taught, and witnessed Him seemingly disregarding the Sabbath to help others, they thought Him a disruptive nuisance and decided to get rid of Him. Jesus, however, was spiritually minded, so He knew the reason they opposed Him was selfish legalism and lust for power. He was also fully aware of *why* He ultimately had to die at their hands.

Like Jesus, you need to engage this spiritual battle for your family from a spiritual perspective, because if you attempt to defend a spiritual attack with a worldly approach you have already lost the battle before you've begun. You cannot fight spiritual battles with carnal weapons. It's like shooting a water pistol into hell, believing you'll douse the flames. In Romans 8:6 we read, "For to be carnally minded is death, but to be spiritually minded is life and peace." For example, when a child's symptoms are staring you in the face, the spiritual battle doesn't make sense to the carnal person—the default is to immediately treat the child with medicine. Yet, despite all the good medicine science has provided, the name of Jesus is much more powerful and effective. *Our* spiritual default, therefore, is the name of Jesus!

Of course, there is absolutely no shame in giving your child medicine if your spiritual ability is not yet at the level needed to defeat a sickness. All believers are still growing their faith, so use your wisdom, applying prayer, faith, and medicine where necessary. Be sure to use the name of Jesus, speak the Word of God over the situation, and lay hands on your child *first!*

Whether your child is sick or not you must speak health over your child every single day.

Develop your spiritual awareness and battle strategy. In time, you will develop the faith required to get your family through any challenge.

Being spiritually minded means that we live in this world in the spirit and are alive to the spiritual. So, don't wait for things to happen! "Death and life are in the power of the tongue" (Proverbs 18:21a), so whether your child is sick or not you *must* speak health over your child every single day.

If you are a Spirit-filled believer you are born into the Spirit of God, so this is your natural place now. Understanding the spirituality of life is where life's purpose resides, and where the victory really is. If you are not a Spirit-filled believer I appeal to you to keep an open mind because I'm going to share some truths that frankly will not only be relevant for your role as a mother, but truths you can extend to all areas of your life.

If you're a new Christian, my desire is to help your walk with God reach a more personal and much deeper level. The sad reality is many Christian women don't know who they are in Christ and so continue to struggle their way through life, without knowledge, tools, and spiritual weapons that will quickly bring them victory. My aim is to make you aware of *who you are in Christ,* and by the time you're done with this book you will be cultured into viewing and living the world from the realm of the Spirit, able to defend your family like a mighty lioness of the tribe of Judah!

Our Tools

The book of Genesis explains that God is the ultimate Creator of everything (Genesis 1:1). In Genesis 2:7 we read about how God formed us from the dust of the ground—our physical component—then breathed into us the breath of life—our spiritual component—providing us with the ability to function in the physical and spiritual realms simultaneously. God also makes a point of telling us He created us in His image and likeness (Genesis 1:26). Now being created in God's image means, like Him, we have also been made creators. This creativity is evident in the magnificent structures and astonishing technology developed through the ages. We stand amazed at what has been made possible through science, especially in the medical field, and yet because it has been accomplished in the physical realm there are limits as to what can be achieved.

Look at it this way, everything in the physical realm was first created in the spiritual realm, so when we live from a spiritual standpoint we are not restricted by the limitations of the physical world. For example, Jesus, who as we know lived with a spiritual perspective, wasn't confined by the natural force of gravity when He walked across a lake to join His disciples (Matthew 14:22-33). Similarly, He healed many from sickness and disabilities with just a word, even raising His dead friend, Lazarus, back to life after four days (John 11:1-43). You may say, "Well, that was Jesus..." but to make my point clear, Jesus Himself said "he who believes in Me, the *works that I do he will do also*; and *greater* works than these he will do" (John 14:12—emphasis mine).

How will we do these greater works Jesus said we would do? Jesus Himself provided the answer to this question a few verses later when He said, "If you ask anything in My name, I will do it" (John 14:14). Jesus' instructions were more specific when He sent His disciples out among the people of Israel: "*He gave them power* over unclean spirits, to cast them out, and to heal all kinds of sickness and all kinds of disease" (Mathew 10:1—emphasis mine), telling them to "Heal the sick, cleanse the lepers, raise the dead, cast out demons" (Matthew 10:8). As these verses state, we have been given the name of Jesus and the power of the Holy Spirit to deal with sickness or disease when we come face-to-face with them.

Please understand that this means we have been delegated divine, legal authority over anything and everything that opposes God's Word. There is no greater authority in eternity than the living God, and you have been given His Name–essentially His signet ring—to use to enforce Heaven's will on Earth. That should get you excited.

As amazing as the advances in medical technology are, they pale in comparison with the spiritual tools we have as New Creation Mothers. I'm not aware of any technology that can heal an illness in seconds the way Jesus did, and certainly nothing that can raise a dead person back to life after four days. The name of Jesus is as good as Jesus being here today. The toolkit a New Creation Mother has is *the all-powerful name of Jesus* against which nothing can stand, the unrivaled wisdom, comfort, and *guidance of God's Holy Spirit*—the very same Spirit who raised Jesus from the dead, and *a mouth to confess* vitality over her family and to pray into the life of each member of her family.

YOUR IDENTITY IN CHRIST

Do you know who you are? I'm not talking about "finding yourself" as the world might say; I'm talking about who you were created to be, and your position in Heaven's rowyal hierarchy? Do you know what you inherited when you made Jesus Christ your Lord? Without this knowledge it is extremely difficult, if not impossible, for us Christian mothers to draw on the inspired will of God in establishing Heaven's will in our world.

I referenced this concept in the previous chapter, explaining that this is only possible by understanding who we are in Christ and by using the formidable weapons and tools at our disposal. Many Christian mothers are hindered by misgivings about their standing in life which usually leads to feeling powerless when it comes to changing the world. All you really need, however, is to start by changing your world, and that starting point is learning who you are in Christ.

So what is your status in this world and what is the potential influence you have on it? In this chapter I will explain your standing as a New Creation Mother, the divine authority afforded by this identity, and the means available to apply this authority.

You Are Brand New

Like Moses feeling unqualified when he was charged with leading his people out of slavery, changing your world may seem like an intimidating and overwhelming task. This is understandable, due to insecurities stemming from our past, old hurts, mistakes made, missed opportunities, and failures. In the Word of God, which is the infallible source of our spiritual instruction, however, we are told:

When you were born again you became a brand new creation; your spirit was recreated with pristine new life.

"Therefore, if anyone *is* in Christ, *he is* a new creation; old things have passed away; behold, all things have become new" (2 Corinthians 5:17). This scripture is not a simple metaphor; what this literally means is when you were born again you became a brand new creation; your spirit was recreated with a pristine new life.

This is reinforced by the statement "old things are passed away," emphasizing the old, sinful nature you once had—the nature that was subject to sickness, disease, death, sin, defeat, and failure—is dead and gone, no longer a part of you. You are a new person, with a brand new life—and I dare say a new name—with *zero* record of the past. The King James Version of the Bible uses the term "new creature" for anyone who has been reborn in Christ, and this term connotes something that is unprecedented, of a new kind, novel, and uncommon[6]. In short, the New Creation Mother you are *now* never existed before![7]

When you became a new creation—a new creature with a new life at the new birth—you were baptized into the Body of Christ, meaning the Church, of which Christ is the head (1 Corinthians 12:13). Your life is now an expression of the beauty and glory of God. His life is in you now, which means you are fully righteous, justified, and saved.

In practical terms, a mother in Christ is one who has her identity in Christ. The life she has is superior to *all* the elements of the world, including sickness, defeat, and any other attack Satan would try to bring against her. As a New Creation Mother you belong in a new class of beings, and as such you must walk in the full consciousness of this new divine life every day. You *permeate* divine life and immortality. You are a master over circumstances with divine dominion over the world's terrible systems. You are powerful and inherently superior to Satan and his cohorts! You must understand your royal identity and begin to use your divine authority to crush the work of Satan, and heal and restore the destruction he has caused in this world.

You Have the Faith of God

The fundamental principle that governs the operation of the Kingdom of God is *faith.* Every other precept in the Kingdom rests on the principle of faith. This is why scripture says without faith it is impossible to please God (Hebrews 11:6). The question is, how do we obtain this faith in order to please God?

The good news is that faith comes by hearing the Word of God (Romans 10:17), so the origin of our faith is the faith that believed in the resurrection of Jesus when we were born again. What I mean by this is our very salvation depended on taking a step of faith, because no person is born-again without faith. Hearing the message of the gospel produces faith for salvation, so when a person hears the gospel—that Jesus died for his or her sins—that person has faith to accept the message and then confesses it in relation to their life, leading to their salvation.

In addition to the faith we exercised to believe the gospel we heard that led to our salvation, we were all also given a measure of faith by God (Romans 12:3b) imparted into our spirit at our new birth. This faith that came to us at salvation came once, is complete, and does not need to be improved upon.

This means all the benefits of salvation are accessed through the faith you received at salvation. So when you hear the Word of God *after* you have received salvation, your eyes are open to what is available to you in the Kingdom of God here on Earth. Salvation is more than just the forgiveness of sins; it is all encompassing redemption, meaning it encapsulates *every single thing* that Jesus came to make available for us in His sacrifice. This is to say your faith for salvation is the faith you use to appropriate provision for every area of your life, including your purpose, healing, financial provision, salvation for loved ones, and every

This faith that came to us at salvation came once, is complete, and does not need to be improved upon.

other need you may have. Yes, that's right—you already have the faith you need for everything and anything.

Knowing now that without faith it is impossible to please God, it follows that when God gave us a measure of faith at salvation He made it possible for us to please Him. This means the believing woman does not need to try to please God—God is pleased with her because of her faith and acceptance of Jesus. The Father loves *us* the same way He loves Jesus, so any worship and giving done in faith is pleasing to God.

You Are Righteous through Christ

To be an effective New Creation Mother it's critical for you to understand you have been made completely righteous through Christ. Romans 1:17 says "the just [righteous] shall live by faith" (parentheses mine). The key to this scripture is that the strength of our faith hangs on our *understanding of righteousness*. Righteousness through faith in Jesus is what brings us peace with God (Romans 5:1).

So, what is righteousness and how do we walk in it through faith? To put it simply, righteousness means being in right standing with God. Contrary to the world's opinion, living a "right" and good life (our own works) doesn't put you in right standing with God. Only accepting Jesus' atoning death on the cross by choosing to be reborn of God's Holy Spirit is what puts you in right standing with God. The crucifixion of Jesus is how God eradicated the sinful nature of man, and in doing so He put us in right standing with Himself. This is an utterly stunning thought when you mull over it for a minute. As 2 Corinthians 5:21 explains, "For He made Him who knew no sin to be sin for us, that we might become the righteousness of God in Him." To be perfectly clear, Jesus *did not* become a sinner; he was *made* sin—*become* denotes a process you enact yourself; *made* is instant, and thrust upon by another. By sending Jesus to die for our sin God dealt with the *nature* of sin that produced the *act* of sin.

Only accepting Jesus' atoning death on the cross . . . is what puts you in right standing with God.

Now listen to this: when Jesus took our sin onto Himself we were not just made righteous… we were made *the righteousness of God*—the very quality of righteousness that God has. Something important to understand is that being righteous is a standing that can be lost, whereas being made the *righteousness* of God is a quality that cannot be lost, improved upon, or diminished in any way. It is also a gift from God.

When your sinful nature was eradicated at your

salvation, it was replaced with the righteous nature of God. A person's identity is their *nature* not their *behavior,* so becoming the righteousness of God is a nature you possess before it becomes an act you carry out. Righteous acts, therefore, should be a natural outcome in your life because you have righteousness as a nature. The believer cannot become unrighteous, even if there are unrighteous acts in her life. The reason many women struggle with acts of righteousness is because they have not realized and understood the nature within them is a righteous nature given by God at their salvation.

Righteous living shouldn't be difficult because we have God's righteousness inherent in us, and this right standing with God affords the new creation mother the ability to function from a position of advantage. This truly makes all the difference in the world for her.

You Have Authority

Authority can only be exercised based on the understanding of that authority, and because many believers have very little idea of the authority they possess in Jesus, they struggle through life. In Colossians 1 Paul speaks of the will of God that has been released and made available to us, saying it pleases our Father when we live in health by His strength (referring to what Jesus has done), and giving thanks to our Father who has

We don't need to ask God to give to us what He has already made available to us.

qualified us to be partakers of the inheritance of the saints (Colossians 1:9-12). This tells us we don't need to ask

God to give to us what He has already made available to us—the authority you have already inherited is the key in your hand.

If you're still not convinced, look at Luke 10:19 in the Amplified Bible. Jesus had just sent his disciples out to practice the works He had been doing, and when they returned they were overjoyed that even the demons were subject to them in Jesus' name. The fascinating part is in this moment, Jesus delegates His authority to them, and by extension He delegated His authority to *you:*

> Listen carefully: I have given you authority [that you now possess] to tread on serpents and scorpions, and [the ability to exercise authority] over all the power of the enemy (Satan); and nothing will [in any way] harm you. Luke 10:19 (AMP)

Understanding the authority you have as a believer begins with knowing your identity in Christ. To explain this let's begin with Jesus as the Son of God. In the New Testament, inheritance followed sonship, so when Jesus was declared a Son He received the nations as an inheritance and the ends of the Earth for His possession (Psalm 2:7-8).

The really exciting part of this is that when Jesus redeemed us by his substitutionary death on the cross we became children of God and joint heirs with Christ (Romans 8:16-17). Paul's letter to the Galatian Church offers more detail on our adopted sonship:

> [4] But when the fullness of the time had come, God sent forth His Son, born of a woman, born under the law, [5] to redeem those who were under the law, that we might receive the adoption as sons… [7] Therefore you are no longer a slave but a son, and if a son, then

an heir of God through Christ. Galatians 4:4-5, 7.

It wasn't only Jesus, however, who entered into the inheritance of all things; *we* too entered into this same inheritance with Him—an inheritance that is incorruptible and does not fade away (1 Peter 1:3-4)! We, therefore, should not have prayer requests for what we have already inherited—health, healing, prosperity, forgiveness of sins. We only need to walk in the light of our inheritance.

Understanding the authority you have as a believer begins with knowing your identity in Christ.

How do we do this? By acknowledging every good thing that is in you in Christ Jesus (Philemon 1:6). All these good things are in you. They are in all believers and we acknowledge them through words. By speaking them. You are entitled and expected to say exactly what God says about you and the authority you have:

> [5] *Let your* conduct *be* without covetousness; *be* content with such things as you have. For He Himself has said, "I will never leave you nor forsake you." [6] So we may boldly say:

> "The Lord *is* my helper; I will not fear. What can man do to me?" (Hebrews 13:5-6)

You will remember in the previous chapter I explained how God created us from the dust of the ground, representing the physical realm, then breathed life into us, representing the spiritual realm, so we could live and operate in both realms *simultaneously*. This becomes really important now in understanding our authority in Christ. In Ephesians 1:20-21 we read how God raised

Jesus from the dead, "and seated *Him* at His right hand in the heavenly *places,* [21] far above all principality and power and might and dominion, and every name that is named, not only in this age but also in that which is to come." A throne represents the seat of authority within a kingdom. Whoever sits on the throne commands the authority in the kingdom. Jesus sits in the seat of the highest position of authority there is, commanding absolute obedience and authority.

The next chapter of Ephesians gets really interesting as it explains how we came to have *our* authority. It tells us that God raised us, His adopted sons and joint heirs with Christ, together with Jesus to sit in the heavenly places with Him:

> [5] Even when we were dead in trespasses, made us alive together with Christ (by grace you have been saved), and raised us up together, [6] *and made us sit together in the heavenly places in Christ Jesus.* Ephesians 2:5-6—emphasis mine.

This scripture makes it unmistakably clear that God raised us up with Jesus to be seated in the heavenly places with Him! Your spiritual seat of authority is not a single millimeter short of sitting with Jesus in His heavenly seat of the highest authority. Consequently, we are seated far above all principality, and power, and might, and dominion, and every name that is named. Along with being seated above all, we also have the authority to use our Lord Jesus' all-powerful name, which has the same impact as Jesus being fully present.

You are a King and Priest

Church and State, or as some put it, "religion" and

"politics," have generally been accepted as separate functions in modern society, and in the entire Old Testament there are only two references to someone who was both a king and a priest. We read of this first royal priest in Genesis 18 where Abram, returning from rescuing Lot and his family from marauding kings, gave a tenth of his plunder to the king of Salem, a high priest of God called Melchizedek. "Now consider how great this man was, to whom even the patriarch Abraham gave a tenth of the spoils" (Hebrews 7:4).

In Psalm 110:4, David is also then declared a priest in a prophetic foreshadowing of the Messiah. Interestingly, David is called a priest after the order of Melchizedek: 'The Lord has sworn And will not relent, "You *are* a priest forever According to the order of Melchizedek."'

There have been many kings and priests since Melchizedek and David, but the next instance of someone being titled a King *and* a Priest is our Savior, Jesus Christ. This is revealed to us from at least two scriptures: in the book of Revelation Jesus is referred to as "The King of kings and Lord of lords" (Revelation 19:16), then the author of the book of Hebrews calls Jesus our High Priest, saying, "where the forerunner has entered for us, even Jesus, having become High Priest forever according to the order of Melchizedek" (Hebrews 6:20), quoting the prophecy in Psalm 110:4.

The role of a priest is to worship and minister to God, to be a mediator between man and God—making intercession with prayer and supplication, and to teach the fundamentals of God's Kingdom. Jesus performs this function perfectly, but I have an exciting revelation for you: today believers hold the same two offices of king and priest as Jesus does, and retain the same spiritual power these offices represent! We know this from Peter's letter to the Church of born again believers when he wrote: "But you are a chosen generation, a *royal priesthood*, a holy nation, His own special people, that you may proclaim the praises of Him who called you out of darkness into His marvelous light" (1 Peter 2:9—emphasis mine).

The term "royal priesthood" in this scripture refers to us as kings (royalty), and priests (ministers of God). As a woman, don't be troubled by the masculine term "king" because this is about the authority the title holds, not the gender. As believers we have the delegated authority of the King of kings over the things of this world, and as a king you will declare a thing and it will be established for you (Job 22:28), meaning when you declare God's will it will be done on Earth as it is in Heaven (Matthew 6:10). This applies to your ministry, your family, your career, and to anything you desire according to the will of Godin your life. As kings we reign in this world and as rulers we decree justice (Proverbs 8:15), so we don't have to accept any corruption or defilement the world tries to push onto us or our family. Kings rule by the authority of their dominion, and absolute obedience to a king's command is required. You can have faith that the forces of darkness *must* obey you when you use your authority.

Priests, on the other hand, offer sacrifices to God and are ordained to receive answers to their prayers. In the Old Testament, bulls and rams were offered as sacrifices (Exodus 29:1), whereas in the New Testament the sacrifices are the praises offered with our lips (Hebrews 13:15). Being priests also provides the authority to bless others through offering them communion.

Consequently, as a royal priest you are a high priest, a ruling priest, and you have dominion and authority to effect any change you need in the world by using the all-powerful name of Jesus.

You Have the Holy Spirit Living Within You

Before Jesus ascended to the Father He promised not to leave us alone, saying He would send another Helper to be with us, who is the Spirit of truth (John 14:16). Jesus then clarified that this Helper is the Holy Spirit who will teach us all things, and remind us of everything Jesus said and promised us (John 14:26). Now it is critical to understand that the Holy Spirit is not some force or wind or mind or angel God sent to be with us; He is the very Spirit of God who was present at the creation of all things (Genesis 1:2) and who adorned the heavens (Job 26:13). He is one with God; a divine member and person of the triune Godhead.

Jesus understood the importance and relevance of the Holy Spirit because the Holy Spirit is the action power of God and was the anointing on Jesus' earthly ministry (John 16:13). When Jesus was baptized by John, the Holy Spirit descended on Him in the form of a dove (Luke 3:22) and led Him into the wilderness to fast for forty days, and be tested by the devil, and defeat every temptation. Then Jesus returned in the power of the Holy Spirit (read the entire chapter of Luke 4).

All the many miracles Jesus did, He performed through the Holy Spirit (John 14:10). By these works it was clear to those around Him that Jesus lived His life and ministry by the Holy Spirit. In fact, in the book of Acts, Luke describes the Holy Trinity at work, plainly for all to see: "how *God* anointed *Jesus of Nazareth* with *the*

Holy Spirit and with power, who went about doing good and healing all who were oppressed by the devil, for God was with Him" (Acts 10:38—emphasis mine).

The best part of Jesus' promise to us is that the Holy Spirit not only dwells *with* us but is *in* us (John 14:17b). It is the Holy Spirit, whom we receive by faith, who helps us to live a fulfilled Christian life. It is the Holy Spirit who carries out the works of God through us as He did through Jesus. It is important to understand that we receive the Holy Spirit by faith at salvation—indeed, He is the one who renews our spirit, however, Jesus spoke of an additional *baptism* into the Holy Spirit with fire (Luke 3:16, Matthew 3:11, Acts 2:1-4). This makes the baptism into the Holy Spirit the single most important requirement after salvation. When you grasp the reality and power of God's Holy Spirit living inside you, it will radically transform how you approach life.

No Christian mother should feel perplexed and disadvantaged when she has the same Spirit who raised Jesus from the dead living in her (Romans 8:11). John 16:13 confirms this: "However, when He, the Spirit of truth, has come, He will guide you into all truth; for He will not speak on His own authority, but whatever He hears He will speak; and He will tell you things to come." This means you do not have to be confused or in the dark about anything because if you allow Him to, the Holy Spirit will guide you with accurate information regarding the circumstances you find yourself in, and He will provide you with a clear strategy to achieve His will in your life. This scripture also says He will reveal the mind of God to you, showing you what is to come. So your future will be planned for and guaranteed with the

Holy Spirit, removing all fears and uncertainties you may have felt.

Romans 8:11 also explains that the Holy Spirit will keep your physical body in health, and *if* there is any sickness He has the ability to make your body well. You only need to receive the revelation that He lives within you, as this enables you to draw on His power. As you practice drawing on His power, you will become more sensitive to the Holy Spirit, especially as you nurture your relationship with Him. We read in Romans 14:17 "the kingdom of God is not eating and drinking, but righteousness and peace and joy in the Holy Spirit." What this means for mothers is that we are not only able to be at peace, overcoming in all areas in a troubled world, but by the Spirit we have the ability to impart the peace we have into the world around us, and in doing so bring others into the Kingdom.

Your Identity in Christ

I think you would now agree that a New Creation Mother's status in society is nothing short of being a *world changer!*

A believing mother is a king and a priest and she takes her ministry of reconciliation very seriously. She claims her inheritance of being seated in heavenly places in the Kingdom. She is aware of, and influences what is happening in her world, and will not be quiet about her God. She is at the forefront of affairs, even if she's not in the pulpit or leading an organization, but in

A New Creation Mother's status in society is nothing short of being a world changer!

her sphere of influence, she's spreading the gospel in some capacity. A New Creation Mother is never complacent but a protagonist for godly change, a royal priest, praying and interceding for transformation, and bringing life to others by the Holy Spirit.

Hallelujah! Isn't that powerful? It gets even better; in the next chapter we'll explore practical ways to effect change in the world in which we operate.

CALLED FOR SUCH A TIME AS THIS

Now that you understand your authority and status as a New Creation Mother, let's begin exploring what benefits you receive when fulfilling this role. This chapter emphasizes how the new creation realities presented in the previous chapter translate into real-world motherhood on different levels. As we progress through the chapter you will be given *practical* examples of what you as a New Creation Mother can do right now to protect your children and your home.

Dangerous Times

When considering what has taken place in countries around the world today, and even the gradual progression in recent decades, I believe it is revealing of what the Bible says about the end times. No matter how we perceive the forces controlling these events, the process is marching forward at a rapid pace. The many freedoms we once cherished are being whittled away on a near-daily basis under the guise of fighting terrorism, prejudice, and infectious diseases. The restrictions imposed on us certainly appear as though governments and big tech, big media, and big pharma companies, seek more and more control of our lives and our children's future. As New Creation Mothers who are now aware of the predicament we face, *and because we recognize* the enemy's strategy, it is up to us to start defending our families against this threat. And there is no time to waste.

Never undervalue the power and authority you carry as a New Creation Mother. This is especially true when you consider how Old Testament women achieved world-changing results *prior to* having the six central principles of our new creation reality available to them. Remember how Rahab became a vital part of God's master plan by acting on her faith. She made a decision to help the Israelites defeat the Canaanites because she was aware of how wicked the culture she lived in truly was, compared with the righteousness she knew was possible under Israel's living God.

Remember as well that Rahab was not exactly a saint but she was what the Bible calls a *harlot.* Yet she had faith and was clearly seeking God's righteousness. I'm sure you understand I don't use Rahab as an example to endorse prostitution but rather to point out that you can start influencing change from wherever you currently are in life. You don't need a platform or large network to make the will of God effective in your world and the world at large. Rahab is, after all, included in the genealogy of Jesus (Matthew 1:5-6)! This just goes to show there is nothing in our own power we can do to please God, especially concerning righteousness. Righteousness is a gift and not received as a result of who we are or anything we do. It's a gift from God received by faith, so simply accept the righteousness of God and start from where you are. It's not about works; it's about your heart and your mind and your commitment to the things of God.

A great example of a woman who was called "for such a time as this" is Esther. She was comfortable, living a luxurious life, and could have ignored the peril facing her people. Through mentorship and council Esther recognized the perilous time she lived in and consequently made herself available to become an agent of change. Even though she was not a biological mother, she became a spiritual mother to the nation of Israel because she was willing to rise up and do the work of God to save her people. Cautioned by her cousin, Mordecai, she realized the Jews were in trouble, so Esther put everything she had on the line to save her people. Think about it, Esther was a queen, she lived in a comfortable palace, and could have easily just brushed aside the danger to Israel and said, "Hey, it won't affect me here in my palace. I'm safe and don't need to be concerned." Yet, she remembered the spiritual implication of complacency.

My point is, even though Esther lived in the physical world, she understood the spiritual consequence of ignoring the looming horrors threatening her people. She looked safe in her physical world, but she took to heart what Mordecai had told her. Mordecai's message, sent to Esther in the palace, said:

> "Do not think in your heart that you will escape in the king's palace any more than all the other Jews. [14] For if you remain completely silent at this time, relief and deliverance will arise for the Jews from another place, but you and your father's house will perish. Yet who knows whether you have come to the kingdom for such a time as this?" Esther 4:13-14

Esther stepped out of her comfort zone to approach the king, thereby risking her life and her position as queen, to save her people. In our busy lives today, the comforts we are tempted to indulge in are things like having TV or social media babysit our children. Even more dangerous is entrusting the vitally important job of preparing our children for adult life to secular school teachers and the modern school curriculum. Modern believers also tend to risk leaving the spiritual health and growth of their children to church youth groups. We all need to honestly consider what areas of our lives must change to ensure the protection of our families. After all, who knows if you have been placed in your role in life *for such a time as this.*

Who knows whether you have come to the kingdom for such a time as this?

Be Conscious of Your Place in Christ

Psalm 91:1 says, "He who dwells in the secret place

of the Most High Shall abide under the shadow of the Almighty." So, what is this secret place? We know in the New Testament, this secret place spoken of is *in Christ.* Christ is a location or a place. We are in Christ. We've been made to sit together with Him in heavenly places (Ephesians 2:6), so this is the place Jesus went to prepare for us, and once we accept His saving grace this is where we now reside. You came into Christ when you were born again; it's a heavenly realm called Zion, the city of the living God. That's the city of our habitation: "But you have come to Mount Zion and to the city of the living God, the heavenly Jerusalem, to an innumerable company of angels" (Hebrews 12:22).

Beyond this, the New Creation mother lives in a place called Christ.

Every Christian lives in a new environment called "Christ." Christ is a person, and Christ is also a place. 2 Corinthians 5:17 says, "Therefore, if anyone *is* in Christ, *he is* a new creation; old things have passed away; behold, all things have become new." This is the environment, and in that environment, we see and live differently; we're alive to God and to the realities of the Kingdom. In that environment we live and prevail by faith; we see with the eyes of the spirit.

Ephesians 2:6 says God has "raised *us* up together, and made *us* sit together in the heavenly *places* in Christ Jesus," which reveals our position of authority. 2 Corinthians 2:14 talks about our life of eternal triumph in Christ. In Christ, you can do all things, and have all things!

When a person is born into this world, they leave their previous environment in the womb, entering into a different environment, and when this happens, things change. You have to live and feed differently now from how you fed in the womb, because of your new environment. It's the same thing spiritually. Now that you're born into Christ, things are different—life is different, and principles are different.

Think of how the Israelites traveled with the atmosphere of Heaven as they wandered in the wilderness for forty years. The glory of God, embodied in a pillar of smoke by day, and a pillar of fire by night, was evidence of the miraculous presence of God with them. They didn't grow out of their clothes and their shoes didn't wear out. They escaped the Pharaoh only to be surrounded by hostile nations, but were kept safe in the atmosphere of God's protection. In similar fashion, the New Creation Mother has the God-given ability to draw on the presence of the Holy Spirit for comfort and protection, and because she is seated in Christ in heavenly places, she is able to create the atmosphere she wants to live in.

Now, some of you may wonder, *How is this possible?* Well, it's quite simple really; within your home, your workplace, or wherever you find yourself, it is possible to be conscious of your place in Christ because you are a new creation who is in right standing with God and you live in the atmosphere of God by being in Christ. A further example is when a person is born into this world: they leave their previous environment in the womb moving into a completely different environment, where almost everything changes. You're fed differently, you're breathing oxygen, you need clothes to remain warm, and more. This is because of your new environment. It's the same thing spiritually. Now that you're born into Christ, things are different; life is different, and the principles are different.

1. Your righteousness came as a result of faith and not through any works on your part. Once you became righteous, you received the authority of a king and priest, living now with the Holy Spirit as your constant guide. So if you ever doubt your ability to influence transformation, remember to trust the Holy Spirit to bring about the changes you desire as He will be working through you. When called to save his people, Moses was full of excuses but God simply reminded him, "I will certainly be with you" (Genesis 3:12).

2. Today God is not only with His new creation, but in us in the person of the Holy Spirit. Never lose sight of the fact that you are filled with God's Holy Spirit, and "with God all things are possible" (Matthew 19:26) when you draw on the strength of the Holy Spirit.

The starting point for being ready for such a time as this goes back to being spiritually minded. A New Creation Mother is a recreated spirit being, and as such she must function from the Spirit in every realm and in every role. Being spiritually minded is crucial because society has set a secular standard—an expectation for wives that we often unknowingly feel obliged to live up to.

When entering marriage, many women—even Christian women—adopt a worldly attitude without realizing it. From literary classics to current social media, we've been made aware of how women have struggled over time; how we've suffered suppression and discrimination through the ages. We hear from friends and read magazine articles about how marriage is not easy, and how we need to be careful to never allow the slightest hint of being dominated by our spouse. We've learned we need to be strong and must stand up for ourselves.

What we don't realize is we're being set up for the *wrong type of conflict* in our relationship.

I can honestly share on this because I have gone through my own drama as a wife. I've lived the conflict I was prepared for going into my marriage. For five years of marriage, my husband and I fought all the time. We argued constantly, and for no good reason. We were evidence that two good people can behave badly, and look bad for no justifiable purpose. Many women enter into their marriage with conflict on their mind, just as I did, telling themselves, "I'm not going to be controlled by any man. I'm going to be strong." We squander our time trying to prove something to those around us, and to ourselves. What we need to do as women, however, is to stop and ask: "Where do I receive the information I'm acting on?" This piercing question points back to the necessity of being spiritually minded in all we do.

What we don't realize is we're being set up for the wrong type of conflict in our relationship.

From a natural standpoint, my concerns were legitimate, and my spouse's concerns were probably legitimate too. At that point, however, neither of us were considering the spiritual legitimacy of our concerns… Everyone wants to be the one who's right, but once I began to spend time in prayer over the situation I realized I was functioning from a position of flesh and pride. I began long periods of praying fervently in the spirit and fasting, and I'm not talking about works here, but the discipline that fasting provides. The outcomes of these periods of fasting really created a humility or brokenness in my spirit.

Many times we enter into prayer with the worldly mindset of "The Lord is going to judge this case, vindicate me, and prove I'm right." Although He will bring you vindication if it is justly required, God won't necessarily do it *your* way. First, He's almost always going to build you and work on you, because He's a God of perfection and wants all to come to repentance and change for the better. During my time of seeking the Lord He showed me I was holding on to an unforgiving mindset, and harboring a lot of bitterness. He knows that changed hearts will lead to peace, and transformation into the likeness of Jesus, so while He may ultimately judge between right and wrong, He functions from Heaven's paradigm, and is not swayed by the standards nor the expectations of the world. What I'm saying is God is primarily concerned with the transformation that comes through fellowship with Him.

What we need to do as women . . . is to stop and ask: "Where do I receive the information I'm acting on?"

One of the things the Holy Spirit was trying to teach me is that I need to spend more time being quiet. I felt Him telling me:

You need to be quiet. You're saying too much. You're trying too hard to prove yourself. Often, even when you have a case, I can't help you because you're all over the place. You need to let go of what's troubling you and truly put your faith in Me, because if you have faith in Me you won't be concerned about what your spouse is doing or not doing...

What I realized during this time of self-reflection is that on most occasions my fear stems from an inadequate level of faith for the occasion. We don't want to admit it, and we often won't admit it! If I'm worrying about my spouse becoming spiritually complacent, or my spouse doing something I won't like, it is a reflection on *my* faith. If I say I'm giving the problem to God, and then take it back by worrying, it only demonstrates fear. If you believe you're a woman of the Spirit, and you can truly make changes, why should you be worried? In fact, scripture instructs us not to be anxious, and to allow God's peace to guard our hearts and minds:

> [6] Be anxious for nothing, but in everything by prayer and supplication, with thanksgiving, let your requests be made known to God; [7] *and the peace of God, which surpasses all understanding, will guard your hearts and minds through Christ Jesus.* Philippians 4:6-7—emphasis mine

You know you have the arsenal; you have the spiritual tools to change things, so start using them.

Some may say I've been brainwashed but the opposite is true. I'm a strong woman in my own right, and I believe I am prepared for such a time as this. I have a strong mind because through the power and wisdom of the Holy Spirit I've become aware of the worldly conditioning that has influenced wives for so long. Even as Christian wives, we've allowed our behavior to be based on the world's system and expectations rather than following what God says about marriage.

We find God's order of marriage in Ephesians 5, where we are told that, as with the Church, Christ is the head of the marriage relationship, and is the example we should follow. Operating in the Holy Spirit, Christ submitted in all things to His Father's will without giving up an iota of His worth (Luke 22:42; John 5:30). In the same way, we can be confident in fulfilling our role as godly wives according to the marriage order ordained by God. As a new creation woman you are a believer—a born again, Spirit-filled firebrand whose actions, when led by the Spirit, will be inspired by the Holy Spirit. You have been made alive to God's Spirit and given royal, divine authority, so in every jurisdiction and in every role you must operate from the Spirit, *especially* in your marriage.

Use What You Have

Being conscious of your place in Christ is by no means limited to your marriage, and must be expanded to your family and your workplace. When approaching life as a career woman, keep your new creation realities in the forefront of your mind—you are brand new so previous errors in judgment are not part of you. You are righteous through Christ and God does not condemn you. You have the mind of Christ and you have everything that pertains to life and to godliness. You have the faith of God so you are able to lead by faith through your ministry or career. You have authority so you are more than a conqueror and an overcomer through Jesus. You have authority to command the will of God as defined by scripture over your business, your department, or the entire company employing you.

You are a king and priest and the Spirit-inspired work you do is a pleasing sacrifice to God, offered in faith.

When confusion or self-doubt try to hinder your efforts, remember you have the Holy Spirit living inside of you and when you seek His guidance, He will ensure you are not confused or in the dark about anything. He will guide you with accurate, scriptural information, and provide the strategy you need to do your work in excellence. The Word of God says it so well: "Trust in the Lord with all your heart, and lean not on your own understanding; ⁶ In all your ways acknowledge Him, and He shall direct your paths" (Proverbs 3:5-6).

This of course does not only apply to corporate employment—these realities apply to New Creation Mothers in any role and at any level of responsibility. Your spiritual arsenal can be leveraged to bring the presence of God into your workplace and your home. This is important because while they're under your covering, your authority in Christ disqualifies any manner of evil from touching your children without your permission, which of course you won't knowingly allow. Childhood illnesses, for example, are on the rise, but I encourage you to *never* be a mother who thinks, *This sickness might be the will of God.* No, it's not. Satan comes to steal, kill, and destroy. Jesus came to give us only life, and life to its fullest (John 10:10, BSB). He demonstrated God's will by healing the sick. I'll be more emphatic: sickness in your family is not the will of God!

If you have a child (or children) battling any sickness or have been given a bad diagnosis, remember that you have the faith of God, *so you have authority* to command the sickness to leave your child's body. Find health/healing truths in the Word of God, and use your authority to constantly insist on those truths and speak to that child's body to align with the truth; and by divine mandate, by divine law, by divine principle, that child's body *must* respond to you and everything you say over it. Good health and divine healing are no longer promises. Christ has already delivered these truths. The believer has health and healing available right *now*.

While changing diapers or dressing your children, tell them, "You have been redeemed from the curse of the Law, which includes sickness and disease. You walk in divine health because Jesus surely bore every sickness and carried every disease; the chastisement of your peace was upon Him and by His stripes you were and are healed" (Galatians 3:13, Isaiah 53:5). When your children are asleep stand over them and declare, "Jesus instructed me to speak to the mountain, therefore I speak to you, sickness, disease, injury, malfunction, and pain, and I command you to be uprooted and cast into the sea! You have no place in my children's bodies. Their bodies function in the perfection within which God created them to function. They are perfect, complete, and lacking nothing in Jesus' name!" (Mark 11:23, James 1:4)[8].

As a New Creation Mother you must confess life and health over your children (whether they are sick or not). I have heard believing mothers speak death over their family by saying things like: "I come from a family where we have a certain type of disease." They're wrong; it doesn't apply to the New Creation Mother's family. You are brand new. You're not part of a family who inherited sickness or disease. You and your children are no longer subject to any family history of sickness, disease, injury, or an adverse mental health condition. You are a new creature with the Holy Spirit living inside you, you have the full authority of a king and a priest, and a spiritual arsenal at your fingertips to live from the realm of the spirit and bring Heaven into your home. Hallelujah!

In the next chapter we will dive deeper into the practical applications of being a king and a priest, discovering when, where, and how, to use this divine authority in your daily life.

A MOTHER, A KING, AND A PRIEST

In the previous chapter you learned that you were born for such a crucial time as this. Hopefully you now comprehend your profound anointing for the task only you can accomplish for God's Kingdom. Now we will dive deeper into understanding the authority of the royal priestly ministry as a New Creation Mother, and how this authority empowers you as a king—literally occupying the same seat of power as Jesus Christ (Ephesians 2:6)—to make decrees and have them carried out.

As we learned in Chapter 2, the book of Revelation makes it clear that when Jesus made us kings He also made us priests, and in doing so, the New Creation Mother is ordained by the King of kings to receive answers to her prayers: "To Him who loved us and washed us from our sins in His own blood, [6] and *has made us kings and priests* to His God and Father, to Him *be* glory and dominion forever and ever. Amen" (Revelation 1:5b-6—emphasis mine).

To function at her peak in her capacity and position as a king, the New Creation Mother must understand the nature and order of her authority. To thrive in her capacity as a priest she must know how to skillfully *wield* her power and be dedicated to a life of prayer. As a king she must be committed to good and righteous governance, justice, and compassion. To reiterate from Chapter 2, don't be troubled by the masculine term "king" because this is about the authority the title holds, not the gender. The book of Romans outlines our position as children of God and heirs with Christ—the highest rank and authority possible in this world: "and if children, then heirs—heirs of God and joint heirs with Christ, if indeed we suffer with *Him,* that we may also be glorified together" (Romans 8:17).

When we take our first position as a believer—being a king and a priest—we step into our God-given authority to make declarations based on the Word of God, and to pray (make requests of God) according to His Word. Below are a few examples of how we can align with God's Word, by boldly speaking His Word in agreement with what He has said concerning us in His Word.

- *Because I have a great High Priest who has passed through the heavens, I will hold fast my confession (saying the same as and affirming what God says). I will therefore come boldly to the throne of grace, that I may obtain mercy and find grace to help in time of need* (based on Hebrews 4:14-16).

- *The Lord has made me the head and not the tail; I am above only, and never beneath, because I heed the commandments of the Lord my God, and I am careful to observe them* (based on Deuteronomy 28:13).

- *I am a woman who excels in her work! I will stand before kings; I will not stand before unknown men* (based on Proverbs 22:29).

- *I have been given the keys of the Kingdom of Heaven, and whatever I bind on Earth will be bound in Heaven, and whatever I loose on Earth will be loosed in Heaven* (based on Matthew 16:19).

Simeon and Anna Recognize Their Redeemer

When Jesus was taken to the temple to be circumcised He was acknowledged as the promised Messiah by two people who had devoted their entire lives to God. The Holy Spirit had revealed to Simeon, a devout man of God very advanced in years and wisdom, that he would see the Messiah in his life time. When the child, Jesus, was brought to him he blessed Jesus and prophesied over His life (Luke 2:25-35). Following this passage, we read about a devout widow and prophetess named Anna who immediately recognized Jesus as the Messiah:

[37] And this woman was a widow of about eighty-four years, who did not depart from the temple, but

served *God* with fastings and prayers night and day. [38] And coming in that instant she gave thanks to the Lord, and spoke of Him to all those who looked for redemption in Jerusalem. Luke 2:37-38

Was Anna specifically praying for the Messiah to be revealed? We aren't given this detail but we do know she was a widow who never remarried, instead spending her life dedicated to God in prayer and fasting. Given this relevant information, it makes good sense Anna's prayers were focused on bringing the Messiah to Israel, and thus was able to recognize the Messiah when He arrived.

Anna was familiar with seeing physical things from a spiritual perspective. There was nothing coincidental about her recognition of the Messiah—there is no other way Anna would recognize Jesus, an infant, except by the Spirit. Similarly, Herod also knew the Messiah had been born, and he too was tuned in to the spirit *he* served—Satan, the deceiver. Simeon, Anna, and Herod were all aware of an important spiritual event that had taken place—the birth of the Christ; the difference is they were looking at it from different spiritual perspectives based on who they served. This is why Anna gave thanks to the Lord, and spoke of Him to all those who looked for redemption in Jerusalem, while Herod decreed that all Hebrew males under the age of two in Bethlehem and in all its districts must be put to death (Matthew 2:16-18).

Because Anna was so spiritually minded, being wholeheartedly immersed in prayer and fasting, it put her in the position to meet her Messiah and gave her the ability to recognize the Savior when she saw Him. As New Creation Mothers we too have the potential to develop this power of spiritual recognition, being made aware of things about our children that only the Holy Spirit could show us. If we remain spiritually minded, God reveals supernatural insights about our children, about the world, and about society around us. For this reason, it's crucial that we stay focused on the spiritual realm rather than on our circumstances or the things of the world.

Simeon and Anna were operating in their priestly ministry to call forth the Messiah, the Savior, and He came. We are in this position now to call forth His return, and we cannot relent from it because Jesus as our High Priest requires the entire world to have heard the gospel before He can return. As our High Priest He intercedes for us, of course, and reigns as our King. All of creation was willed to Him, and we share in

If we remain spiritually minded, God reveals supernatural insights about our children, about the world, and society around us.

His inheritance yet also carry the responsibility of being His voice, as well as His hands and feet. We wear the same title and position as our Lord Jesus, except He's in Heaven and we're here on Earth. We're His heavenly department on Earth; His representatives and ambassadors (2 Corinthians 5:20) carrying out the remainder of His work.

Changing Your Physical Reality through Your Spiritual Understanding

Another outstanding example of a woman who put all her trust in God is Hannah, the mother of Samuel, who grew to become a pivotal figure in Israel's history. Hannah's story is one of suffering and sacrifice. Taunted by her husband's other wife because she couldn't have children, Hannah begged God to bless her with a son, vowing to give him to the service of the Lord (1 Samuel 1:11). God heard her prayer and blessed her with a son who she named Samuel. Keeping her vow, once he had been weaned she brought Samuel to Eli the priest. Hannah made Samuel a little robe every year and brought it to him when she came up with her husband to offer the yearly sacrifice (1 Samuel 2:19). Upon seeing them Eli would bless Hannah and her husband saying, "The Lord give you descendants from this woman for the loan that was given to the Lord" (1 Samuel 2:20).

There is an important detail regarding Hannah's devotion to God that is not to be overlooked: after releasing Samuel to Eli in dedication to the Lord, "the Lord visited Hannah, so that she conceived and bore three sons and two daughters. Meanwhile the child Samuel grew before the Lord" (1 Samuel 2:21). This significant detail reflects God's kindness toward those who seek Him. From being barren and tormented, Hannah was blessed beyond measure with an abundance of children. Her son, Samuel, whom she dedicated to God, would also prove to become a judge, as well as one of Israel's greatest prophets.

Hannah serves as a good example for women who might be mothers-in-waiting. Perhaps you're dealing with infertility issues, or for whatever reason you're finding it difficult to become pregnant. Hannah chose not to focus on her situation but rather prayed and fasted to change her physical reality through her spiritual understanding. Hannah trusted God to give her a son and by faithfully honoring the promise she made to Him, her blessings increased exponentially. Many women would be tempted to say, "This child is mine and I will determine his future. After all, I waited a long time to have him." Hannah, however, didn't prioritize her own desires over her vow. Instead, she continued in the Spirit and gave her only, long-awaited, child back to God. A testament to the assurance of God's healing power is Hannah's other five children born after Samuel. When the Lord heals, He heals completely!

Don't be swayed by what you feel or see if it seems as though nothing is changing despite your daily declarations, rather look to God's Word and hold on to the certainty that you will receive everything you confess in alignment with His Word: "Let us hold fast the confession of *our* hope without wavering, for He who promised *is* faithful" (Hebrews 10:23).

The Same Yesterday, Today, and Forever

Reading about women of faith in the Bible who changed their circumstances or those of their family is encouraging, but are women achieving similar results in their position as priests today? I can say with certainty that there are, and I have listed a couple of examples below of where these testimonies can be found.

Author, Deborah McDermott has written a book revealing how a believing mother is able to tap into God's miraculous healing power. Deborah's confessions of faith released the power of God to have both her sons healed of autism in *Autism Healed: One Woman's Fight to Save Her Sons*[9]. Another great book, *Hope for a Healed Child: One Mother's Daring Journey of Faith*[10], is authored by Mara De Los Reyes, and details how she stood on God's Word to ensure "Vaccine injury would not have the last word" over her infant son's life.

Reading the faith journeys of fellow believing women gives us a glimpse into what is possible when we stand strong in faith, confessing the Word of God over our lives. It also can provide practical tools to apply to specific aspects of our lives. Dodie Osteen's book, *Healed of Cancer*[11] is yet another example of how we can "download" a blueprint scenario created by a fellow believer and apply it to our own life. The examples provided display how people living on Earth today can uplift us and build our faith, especially because their stories are current and they relate to the modern world around us.

As Hebrews 13:8 tells us, "Jesus Christ *is* the same yesterday, today, and forever," so reading these relatable stories about how modern people apply biblical concepts is a good way to bolster our faith because as much as we may strive to be spiritually minded, we still have the tendency to focus on what we see in the natural world. Seeing how other modern women apply God's Word to difficult circumstances helps us to not only recognize biblical truths, but to then actually apply them to our own lives.

The importance of prayer, declarations, and affirmations cannot be overemphasized. Praying for and confessing life over our children must be prioritized if they are to overcome the world's wicked systems put in place to sway them from the truth. I urge you to read God's Word consistently and seek out scriptures applicable to your life and those you love, and speak them over your family and circumstances. There are some wonderful resources that have been compiled to guide you in this process.

Emily Preston is a believing woman who has created a list of confessions on her site called *Faith Talks*[12] covering critical aspects of the human journey (divine health, finances, wisdom, freedom from depression, and much more). It's a free online resource and I encourage you to make use of this treasure trove of scriptural confessions. As New Creation Mothers we must constantly confess God's Word over our children and our families, and Emily Preston offers some valu-

The importance of prayer, declarations, and affirmations cannot be overemphasized.

able confessions for specific topical situations. Another great resource is a pair of books offered free on the Christ Embassy website called *Faith's Proclamations for Healing & Health vol 1&2*[13] by Pastor Chris Oyakhilome.

Dead Raised to Life

In the eleventh chapter of Hebrews we are reminded of how, by faith, a host of biblical heroes overcame the trials they endured. We are told that "by faith the walls of Jericho fell down," and that "the harlot Rahab did not perish with those *who did not believe*" (Hebrews 11:30-31—emphasis mine). The passage goes on to mention renowned biblical heroes of faith, but the final point made in this passage is perhaps the most powerful, and certainly pertinent to this book: "Women received their dead raised to life again" (Hebrews 11:35). This specifically refers to two women in the Old Testament, whose children were restored to life. These instances can be found in 1 Kings 17:19-24 and 2 Kings 4:18-37.

While it was undoubtedly both Elijah and Elisha's spiritual awareness that played a role in raising these children from the dead, the women certainly played their part by putting their faith in God to work a miracle. These were two mothers who didn't necessarily exercise good judgment all the time. They didn't always get it right and probably lost their temper on occasion. What we do know is they were regular women who received their children back to life through exercising their faith. There is no limit to what a New Creation Mother can do *if she seeks first the kingdom of God and His righteousness,* because then all these things shall be added to her (paraphrase of Matthew 6:33). So, *I dare you* to have faith. To be a woman of faith; to live a life of faith and see the results. A woman who lives a life of faith can bring anything back to life, whether it's a dying dream, a dead career, a dead marriage, or ailing parents.

I dare you to have faith. To be a woman of faith; to live a life of faith and see the results.

With the authority a New Creation Mother has as a king and a priest, she can expect to receive whatever is dead raised to life again. The key point to remember is that *faith is a spiritual activity.* When Rahab put her faith in the God of Israel to save her family, God didn't judge her by who she was or what she had done. James explains it this way: "Likewise, was not Rahab the harlot also justified *(made righteous)* by works *(of faith)* when she received the messengers and sent *them* out another way?" (James 2:25—parentheses mine). This is a vital concept to grasp—faith is a spiritual activity put into practice by applying it to the circumstances we want to change in the physical world.

Any believing woman, any believing mother, has this ability if she aligns with the Word of God, and if she chooses to actively walk the path of faith. For those who might be judging themselves, saying, "Maybe I'm not qualified…" No! If you have made Jesus Christ your Lord, you are qualified as a joint heir to His inheritance— you wear the mantle of a priest, and you have the authority of a king. Just make up your mind to use what you have learned. You *are* qualified. You *have* the authority. Begin to put it to work. Just do it. My message to you as a New Creation Mother and a priest is this: "The word of the Lord in your mouth *is* the truth" (1 Kings 17:24). I like the way Pastor Chris Oyakhilome says it in his book referenced above, "The word of God in your mouth is God talking." Begin speaking the Word of the Lord over your family today and see the results manifest.

RAISING GODLY CHILDREN

This chapter is perhaps the most crucial of the entire book. If you want your children to be game-changers in *their* realm of influence it is vital that you instill godly values into your children. These values will give them a foundation to continue searching for, and discovering, God's will for their lives. We must un-

There is no junior Holy Spirit . . . the same Holy Spirit who raised Jesus . . will work through children.

derstand that children are never too young to pray for other children and influence their lives in a godly way. There is no junior Holy Spirit for children; the same Holy Spirit who raised Jesus from the dead will work through children with as much power as He does through adults…. but you need to steward this tremendous responsibility correctly.

You Are God's Steward

As a New Creation Mother you have a specific assignment in raising your children—you are a steward over your children, who primarily belong to God. Recognizing this is crucial, because when you understand your role as steward you will raise your children according to *God's plan* rather than your own inferior plan. You will dedicate time and energy into raising them according to godly principles, relying on the Holy Spirit to receive specific direction for each of your children. God knows each of your children intimately, so the Holy Spirit will work through you to ensure the foundation for His perfect plan for each child's life is properly established.

Proverbs 22:6 spells out our mandate as mothers and provides a promise following our obedience: "Train up a child in the way he should go, And when he is old he will not depart from it." Your home should be your child's first introduction to the kingdom of God and ministry. Church starts in the home, so taking your children to a physical location called church should be a continuity of what is already happening in the home but with the added blessing of fellowship among a community of believers. It's not enough for a child to be born in a Christian home, you must be intentional in your approach to every child's spiritual education. When a child is born into a Christian home the child has a great advantage, providing them a wide range of possibilities, but don't assume that because you run a Christian home in name alone, your children will learn godliness on their own. It just doesn't work that way. Children learn by example, so whatever you *do* they will emulate.

Even before a child is able to understand teachings at children's church you can start training them in the way of the Lord. Teach your children to pray correctly (to God, in the name of Jesus) from when they are able to talk. Lead by example and encourage them to approach God directly. Read to them from the Bible consistently, and make sure they have a children's Bible of their own even before they can read. Start them out with a picture Bible so they familiarize themselves with the stories and characters that bring God's Word to life. It is vital that you take your children to church consistently, teaching them the importance of fellowship and getting into the Word from a very young age. Meet them at their level. Guard against thinking these things are too advanced for kids—never underestimate children, thinking they won't "get" it. They *will* get it. They get everything else… they get everything else that the world has to offer unless we teach them to reject it. It's mainly in Christian circles that you hear people say, "Will a child grasp this information? Will they get it?" Yes, they will—*if* you model it as the fruit of the Spirit.

So what is the scriptural basis and blueprint for raising children in a godly home? Based on a passage from 2 Corinthians, the believing mother must *intentionally* reconcile her children with God. Every believer has been reconciled with God through Jesus and is then called into the ministry of reconciliation by the Father, so your children are no different:

> [18] Now all things *are* of God, who has reconciled us to Himself through Jesus Christ, and has given us the ministry of reconciliation, [19] that is, that God was in Christ reconciling the world to Himself, not imputing their trespasses to them, and has committed to us the word of reconciliation.

> [20] Now then, we are ambassadors for Christ, as though God were pleading through us: we implore *you* on Christ's behalf, be reconciled to God. 2 Corinthians 5:18-20

The process of reconciling the world to God must start

It is your duty as a New Creation Mother to prepare your home so the precious seed in your care will be raised in fertile spiritual soil.

with your own children. This means leading and pointing them to Christ from a young age, and creating an environment within your home favorable to raising godly children. In the Parable of the Sower Jesus distinguished between different types of ground where seed might fall— some by the wayside, some on stony ground, and some among thorns, but all these seeds perished (Mark 4:3-7). The fourth type of ground Jesus mentions is fertile, able to produce an excellent harvest: "But other *seed* fell on good ground and yielded a crop that sprang up, increased and produced: some thirtyfold, some sixty, and some a hundred" (Mark 4:8).

It is your duty as a New Creation Mother to prepare your home so the supremely precious seed in your care—

your children—will be raised in fertile spiritual soil.

When Jesus was alone with His disciples later that day, He explained the meaning of the parable: "But these are the ones sown on good ground, those who hear the word, accept *it,* and bear fruit: some thirtyfold, some sixty, and some a hundred" (Mark 4:20). As the passage instructs, however, your children must first effectively *hear* the Word before they can *accept* it and thereafter *bear fruit*. The New Creation Mother can raise her children to follow God by *intentionally* creating fertile soil within her home to produce godly children.

All too often, many parents think it is okay to focus only on a child's physical needs, hoping the child will make a decision to follow God at some point in their life. Especially in these end times, however, we can't just leave such a crucial decision up to chance and coincidence, because today's children are being targeted at every level: spiritually, physically, and mentally. The simple truth is you *have* to intentionally train up your children in the way of the Lord.

We live in an era where the spiritual reciprocal of this action is scarily true: there is intentionality about seizing your child's attention and destiny for satanic destruction. Like it or not, or whether you're aware of it or not, we're engaged in a brutal spiritual war over our kids right now. Where chance may have worked in the past, it will no longer work now. When a child comes to you and says, "I have a headache," what is your default response? Is it, "Let me look for some headache tablets in the cabinet," or will you ask the child, "Have you spoken the Word over yourself? Have you spoken to the headache? Have you told it to leave?" This is the kind of response that must flow naturally from your lips in these situations. I do this with my children to make sure they are given the opportunity to hear the Word, accept it, and then bear fruit.

I was having my hair done at a Muslim lady's house one day and noticed she had children who were younger than my first two—their ages were eight and six years old

A child should be taught to automatically consider the question, "What does God's Word say about this?"

respectively. All of a sudden, their dad came out of the bedroom dressed in his full *salat* (Islamic prayer) regalia, and the kids scrambled to fulfill the process they had been taught. They rushed off to go wash their hands and their feet because they were getting ready for prayer. Once the children had performed their necessary cleaning rituals, their father pulled out a mat, and the little boy went to stand next to his dad to say their prayers to Allah. It was obvious those children knew the drill, and it was evident they all prayed frequently throughout the day. I couldn't help but be impressed by that scenario and at the same time, it made me realize Christians need to rapidly up their game.

Truly, this isn't complicated, but it does take an intentional plan. We need to model the effective Christian lifestyle to our children from birth. When they are old enough, we shouldn't have to ask them, "Have you prayed today? Have you read your Bible?" These actions should be their default actions; the things they do naturally without being prompted. A New Creation Mother should be constantly explaining the ways of the Lord to her children, and helping them to go about their daily tasks with the spiritual realm in mind. It is our duty to teach them the good and fruitful life that comes from hearing and acting on the Word of God. In every circumstance of life, a child should be taught to automatically consider the question, "What does God's Word say about this?"

To recap, some basic first steps are:

1.   Ensure that your home is an extension and reflection of the kingdom of God and of Heaven.

2.   Train your children to know the Word, speak the Word, and *do* the Word.

3.   Cultivate them in the habit of going to church.

4.   Ensure they are involved in church and godly activities.

5.   Introduce them to the ministry of the Holy Spirit and using the name of Jesus.

Again, it is vital that *you* are the example to your children in all these areas. Are you displaying faith to your children or are you displaying fear? As in the example previously given, when your child tells you he or she has a headache, the biblical and spiritual approach must be built into their heart and mind.

Of course, I must add the necessary disclaimer here: please don't misunderstand me when I say you should teach your child to *pray first* over a headache or any other illness—it is certainly the first thing they must do, but this doesn't mean as a believer you're against using medicine. This is not at all what I'm saying. The truth of the matter is some people, including children, may need medicine, especially if they have not yet developed their faith to the degree where they can believe for their healing or to live in divine health. These people may well need some medical intervention, and that's perfectly okay, but it shouldn't be the first line of defense. A spiritual approach must be the first line of defense and the shield of protection over your family as you grow your faith in small, incremental steps (Mark 4:28).

In addition, my aim is not to place any mother under condemnation because it is not wrong to use medication, but if you are interested in growing spiritually and teaching your children to do the same, there needs to be a balance between developing your faith and using medicine when necessary as you grow. Again, please don't take this idea out of context—administer whatever medicine may be needed, but teach your child to pray first and to trust God for their healing and divine health. Remember, how you live your life will affect your children. Children should be well versed in the ways of God. They learn this by example, watching their parents and putting into practice whatever they say and do.

A New Creation Mother must not only teach her children to pray and confess the Word over themselves but she should also be praying and confessing God's Word over them. You can't tell your children to pray three times a day but you're sitting watching television while they're praying. If they don't see you praying and hear your heartfelt prayers, how will your children even know you're a believer, let alone vouch for your Christianity?

We are their first teachers and instructors, so what you're teaching them is what they will grow up saying and doing. If I'm not intentional about telling my child the importance of praying, reading the Bible, and carrying out godly activities, then where exactly will they learn these things? Someone will undoubtedly teach them a doctrine—of this you can be assured! In this day and age, you want to make sure it is *you*, rather than their friends, the TV set, or YouTube. This is important to set them up for a life of faith, and to transform them into mountain-movers and world-changers!

Draw Out Their Potential

Consider the circumstance in which Jesus performed His first miracle. He had never done anything miraculous before turning water into wine. Mary, Jesus' mother, was well aware of His divine personhood and almost certainly His potential power, so she encouraged Him to use it. Reading the text of John 2:1-11, it seems Mary put her Son on the spot at the wedding in Cana. When they ran out of wine, Jesus' mom said to Him, "They have no wine" (John 2:3). The response Jesus gave to His mother was, "Woman, what does your concern have to do with Me? My hour has not yet come" (John 2:4). His mother's reply was priceless! Mary simply "said to the servants, 'Whatever He says to you, do *it.*'" It certainly seems Mary encouraged her Son to draw on His power—she expressed a physical need that she knew He could meet if He chose to engage the spiritual realm.

You see, Mary understood her son's divine calling so she was addressing Him based on that. She did not address Him as only a carpenter's son whose prime calling was learning how to build furniture. Mary knew the mission and the purpose of her child, so she focused on addressing the spiritual destiny contained within Jesus. When she prompted Him to do this miracle, however, Jesus even protested and told her it wasn't His time but His mother ignored this and called something out of Him. Even though He said His time had not yet come, He still performed the miracle because Mom expected it of Him. I think this is one of the most interesting details in the Bible.

Mary persuaded Jesus to apply Himself to the evident need. She wouldn't take no for an answer, and she is the model we can emulate—we must understand each child's destiny, and give our children the same encouragement; the same gentle persuasion. Get started. Let your children know the power that exists within them—literally the same power that raised Jesus from the dead (Romans 8:11). Pray for your children. Draw God's power out of them. Don't wait for them to get older. *Now* is the time because you're the leader and there is a limited window of time to instill this mindset within them. If you're married, enlist the help of your husband if he isn't leading the charge already. Make it a joint effort. Nothing cements a concept in a child's mind like seeing their parents united over it. You won't always have this precious window of time.

I talk to a lot of parents every day, some with children who are well passed their formative years and already approaching adulthood. At this late stage the parents start planning for their children, wishing and hoping they will become whatever the parents want them to be… but often, the sad truth is that it's a little too late for what these parents are hoping their children will achieve. When your child is approaching adulthood you may have missed your moment in time.

A friend told me he read about a father who measures the influence he has on the lives of his children by calculating how many days he has left to teach them necessary life skills. He may have two thousand days left to train up his children, for example, so every year as the days wind down, he knows exactly how many days he has left to influence his children. Once they reach eighteen or nineteen years old and they leave the family home, he has to rely on influencing them from a distance, at which point they're living by what they've been taught. So he has to do as much as he can to teach them everything they need to know as early as possible. He gives himself a schedule so he knows how much time he has left to cultivate godly wisdom in their life.

Feed Your Child's Spirit

In this section I'll start by asking, "What part of your child are you addressing? Are you feeding their flesh or are you feeding their spirit? For example, are the summer plans you arrange for your children Spirit-led?" The summer break is generally focused on fun, and fun is good, but *will they grow* in spiritual maturity through the activities you arrange for them? Think about where you place your children for the summer break because sometimes the summer camps our children attend are not beneficial for them spiritually, to say the least.

What part of your child are you addressing? Are you feeding their flesh or are you feeding their spirit?

We should be thinking about taking kids where the lessons and activities will be pouring godly substance into their spirits. For example, in Kansas City there is a group of people who run twenty-four-hour prayer campaigns who have also established an event called *Signs and Wonders Camp*[14]. As well as the camp being an opportunity for children to travel and see new places, the camp facilitators will be pouring biblical wisdom into the spirits of the children who attend. They still have a good time but their spirits are well fed, and these vacation times have an added advantage because the children are free from the pressures of school and school events, so it's a great time to really build spiritual discipline into them.

The goal is to make sure your children know the Lord for themselves and want to be in constant fellowship with their Father, God. They must look forward to children's church and enjoy the time they spend there. If they don't like the children's church where you fellowship, you either need to get involved in the children's church to bring about any necessary change or you must find another church where your kids enjoy attending. Your involvement, however, goes beyond just children's church. You have to pay attention to the Word your child is receiving into his or her spirit every day. The truth of the matter is that many of our youth and children's church ministries are not resourced well-enough and it is often difficult for the youth leaders to follow up with every child. You also obviously want to look for ministries that put special focus on being intentional about the Word of God, because if a ministry is not intentional about the Word of God in the adult church, it's almost certainly not going to be intentional in the youth and children's church ministries.

To be frank, many typical American churches have a rather mundane curriculum. Not even the most basic scriptural concepts are being taught. Children are not being taught to confess the Word, nor how to pray. These are fundamental elements of our faith that I believe children should start learning from a very young age. I don't expect children to recite the Bible from cover to cover, but a subject like the believer's authority is honestly one that children should be taught as part of a standard Christian curriculum. Every child should learn this from the beginning of their walk with God so they can grow their effective, biblical faith in confidence. There is no better time to teach it than at that young, impressionable age. The believer's authority, types of prayer and their use in the appropriate scenarios, and the application of faith to daily life, should really be part of a standard curriculum for children.

New Creation Mothers in many ways truly hold the power of their children's future, especially because children readily believe what adults tell them, and the mother often spends the most time with the children. Just think about how excited kids become when the subject of superheroes comes up, or when they have a Marvel movie to watch with a range of characters who have awesome powers. If children believe these fantasy characters are real, why would they not believe they too have superpowers to lay hands on the sick? To raise their family or friends off a sickbed and pray life into them to bring about a full recovery from any illness? Children have natural faith because they trust the word of an adult, so how much more will they trust God's Word when we bring it to life for them? In truth, children have such great natural faith, Jesus said in Matthew 18:3: "Assuredly, I say to you, unless you are converted and become as little children, you will by no means enter the kingdom of heaven."

A child's impressionability is yet another reason I think it's so important to have Spirit-led, faith-filled individuals who are given to prayer and the ministry of the Word teaching in children's church. Any children's teacher has enormous influence over these young lives because they wholeheartedly believe what you say, which gives teachers a greater responsibility. The Bible informs us teachers have a higher responsibility: "My brethren, let not many of you become teachers, knowing that we shall receive a stricter judgment" (James 3:1). Why is this? When you're teaching God's Word, you can't afford to get it wrong because you can mislead people. I think teaching children carries even greater responsibility because adults are capable of weighing what they have been told, but kids usually just accept the word of an adult at face value. They believe what you say. In fact, Mark 9:42 (NIV) covers this (and more): "If anyone causes one of these little ones—those who believe in me—to stumble, it would be better for them to have a large millstone hung around their neck and to be drowned in the depths of the sea."

For this reason, it is critical that the children's church they attend is following the Word and teaching the *effective power* of the Word, not watering scripture down by teaching things like: "Because God loves everybody everyone will automatically enter Heaven." Children need to know the truth. What I am saying is make sure the children's church your child attends is not a babysitting service—it must be an *actual* church service for children, introducing them to the spiritual fundamentals that will build a strong foundation of faith.

A CALL TO ACTION

Now let us get down to brass tacks; in this day and age Christian mothers cannot take for granted any area relating to their family's lives. Too often a mother has no idea of what her children are doing when they are out of her sight. She is blind to what they're watching at a friend's home, the values, beliefs, and attitudes they are being exposed to at school, as well as the messages embedded in the music they listen to. It is imperative we be proactive and pay attention to what is influencing our children instead of waiting to react when things spin out of control. Understand that the enemy is cunning and subtle in his approach, and resisting him early and often is vital for the safety of our families. It is up to us—New Creation Mothers—to be mindful of the schemes and devices used to gain access to the minds and hearts of children.

You *need* to come to the realization there is an enemy on the loose and that this enemy does not fight fair. You  have learned your identity in Christ, and now that you know these truths and the alarm has been sounded, I must emphasize the *responsibility* you have to your family and your world as a believing woman. The time is now! You have God-given authority to go out and find sick people to pray for and heal, to speak to your child's school system, to evangelize, and to conform your world to God's will.

It is imperative we be proactive and pay attention to what is influencing our children.

It may sound radical but until we begin to behave this way we're not going to make any meaningful change in the areas over which we have influence. A police officer is just a regular person, but when you see a police officer in uniform, you immediately recognize the authority presented by the officer's badge and uniform. In the same way, when your behavior reflects the spiritual authority you carry, circumstances and situations affecting your life and your family will be influenced in a supernatural way.

This chapter is about the practicality of implementing what I learned from choices I made in my life, and to encourage you to avoid making the same mistakes. I will offer some examples from my own life on decisions I've had to make, and how, having learned by the missteps

I've made, I had to go back to correct those decisions.

When a person tries to motivate or comfort someone else it's more readily accepted if they have been through a similar situation or experienced a comparable heartache. It's like when you're deciding on a trip, a travel agent is helpful in recommending destinations from which they have heard a good report, but when you're on the actual journey, a local guide who has been where you are going is far more valuable. The reason I say this is, I am a woman of faith *because* I have had times when I tried it my own way and I paid heavily for it. I've learned to stand on my faith after making these mistakes, so I speak from experience.

I have used my faith for my own body when I suddenly became ill and all the medical imaging available to me could not find the problem. I used my faith to shift my status from broke to rich. When two family members and a friend were separately diagnosed with chronic—possibly terminal—illnesses, I used my faith to keep them alive. I have successfully prayed in faith for sick children's healing who were given lifelong diagnoses, and I have used my faith to bring forth my third child after being proclaimed infertile by the doctor.

As a mother I have learned how the enemy we face offers no sympathy for innocence or ignorance. Scripture states this very clearly: "Be sober, be vigilant; because your adversary the devil walks about like a roaring lion, seeking whom he may devour" (1 Peter 5:8). In defense of his attacks we are advised to "Put on the whole armor of God, that you may be able to stand against the wiles of the devil" (Ephesians 6:11). As kings, priests, and mothers we need to stand up and take action against a world trying to disrupt our family, draw our children away from God, and interfere with the plan He has for their lives.

Don't Be Part of the Problem

When my husband and I decided we wanted to have a third child we prayed about it. We knew it was the will of God—we were in agreement, we knew it would be a boy, we had a name chosen for him, dreams for his life, and everything that accompanies being blessed with a child. The only thing holding us back was that I just didn't fall pregnant. After trying for some time, even though I hadn't needed to when we had our other children, I decided to go to the doctor to see why we were finding it difficult to have this child.

It seemed like a good, logical thing to do, but we sometimes don't realize the consequences of acting in the flesh, according to our emotions, versus being spiritually minded *at all times*. As a believing woman working with the Holy Spirit, I should rather have relied on the Holy Spirit for direction and guidance on this matter, especially since I was convinced it was in line with His will for our family. The result of this decision was that after performing the required tests, the doctor had bad news for us. He told us I had a condition called polycystic ovary syndrome. This syndrome causes secondary infertility, which is the inability to become pregnant or to carry a baby to term after having previously given birth.

We sat there devastated as the doctor explained our options and prescribed fertility medicines. We had the prescriptions filled but suddenly something within me was not convinced about moving forward with this plan. The more I looked at the medicines I had bought, the more I prayed about the situation we were in. I did not want to take the fertility shots, so I prayed and adamantly began to stand on God's Word. What started out as the simple desire to have a third child had suddenly turned into a scary journey, but while I was tempted to follow the doctor's advice and take the medicine prescribed, something within me was just not convinced. This led to realization that in spite of being tempted to listen to the doctor, I must *choose* rather to listen to the Word of God.

I knew God was in agreement with me having another child, "and being fully convinced that what He had promised He was also able to perform" (Romans 4:21), I chose to stand on His Word until Christian, our third child and beautiful son, was born. Please understand, I am not saying conception with intervention is wrong, but at my faith level I knew it wasn't necessary for me. I had been tempted to discount God's Word in favor of man's but God is ever-faithful and He strengthens us to endure any temptation:

> No temptation has overtaken you except such as is common to man; but God is faithful, who will not allow you to be tempted beyond what you are able, but with the temptation will also make the way of escape, that you may be able to bear it. 1 Corinthians 10:13

I started trusting God and retraced my steps, which led to a decision made by faith *not* to rely on fertility medicine. I put my faith in God, and He gave me the final victory.

The point I'm making is many times *we* are the cause of our problems. If you're not careful about the decisions you make—in my case not relying totally on the Holy Spirit to guide me—you may open the door for the enemy and compound the problem. I should have continued relying on the Spirit in everything leading up to the birth of this child. The reality I eventually grasped from this event is that in the journey of faith you have to come to a place of being *fully* persuaded even when it looks like things are not going as planned. Keep standing and continue walking the path of faith; do not be double minded or start looking for other options. Stay the course because even though we can't see the things for which we are believing, they are *real*; they *have* substance: "Now faith is the substance of things hoped for, the evidence of things not seen" (Hebrews 11:1).

Be Part of the Solution

People seem genuinely confused about simple issues like what a parent's scope of responsibility is regarding their children, and what the role of a teacher or coach is. I found a very obvious example of this issue while reading an article, in which a mom was saying children should be taught in school how to be polite and say, "Yes ma'am" or "Yes sir" when addressing an adult. I disagree! This sort of basic training must start at home. The lessons learned at home can be reinforced at school but elementary responsibilities like raising polite children should definitely start at home. We've discussed the danger of social media and technology through which our children have access to worldly viewpoints and values if we don't watch over and guide them. There are far too few barriers in place to filter out the anti-biblical worldviews that dominate social and mainstream media, so it's our responsibility as New Creation Mothers to counteract this orchestrated drive to influence our children.

As a priest you have the responsibility of interceding for your family and ensuring life and godliness are established in your home. Intercession and intervention are required in all areas of your home so you must exercise your authority and confess the life promised in God's Word over your children, rather than accepting and confessing what the world decides is a fitting label. Our adversary, the devil, understands that you must confess something with your mouth to make it become a reality, and he employs many subtle ways to get you speaking harm or failure into existence. One of these ways is evident in how the principalities at work in our world lure you into partnering with them to destroy your very own child. When a child is given a negative diagnosis, the secular pressure is strong to persuade you into joining them by using their labels when describing your child's symptoms or behavior.

When you allow the world to diagnose your child and then placidly accept the diagnosis, you are bound to keep repeating it on cue, giving your stamp of divine authority to that diagnosis. When someone asks after your child's health, don't revert to the clinical words used to describe your child, saying, "Oh, he has terrible allergies." Rather confess life and health over your child with a response from God's Word: "He is healed and whole by the stripes of Jesus" (1 Peter 2:24). Never forget that "death and life are in the power of the tongue" (Proverbs 18:21), so what you confess over your family will come to pass. Who cares if people think you're weird? They already do, so why not have a healthy child as well? Christian mothers tend to think, *We're in God's hands so we'll just sail along and see how it goes...* This is no way to enforce your child's God-ordained destiny, nor is it any way to prepare your children with the biblical worldview they need to accomplish that destiny. As a mother you have to be fully proactive in your child's life.

So pray consistently (without ceasing) over your children. Pray at all times during your day. Of course, you should schedule times of prayer, but you can pray at any time throughout the day as well. When you're in your kitchen, use the time to declare the Word of God over your family with confessions like, "My children are strong in the Lord and in the power of His might. They walk in obedience to God; they keep His Word and they prosper in all they do and wherever they go" (based on Ephesians 6:10, 1 Kings 2:3). As a New Creation Mother, be conscious of your spiritual life and live under the guidance of the Holy Spirit at all times. Don't see things at face value and think *Oh, it's just a cold, it has to run its course*—No! See it for what it is—an attack on your family—and drive it out before it can take hold. Sickness is from hell. It's as simple as that.

Taking responsibility for your children's spiritual and physical wellbeing extends to all areas of their life, even to selecting schools for them. Before my son was even of school age—when he was about two years old—I felt a leading that I needed to pray and ask God about the school he would attend; the specific school the Lord wanted me to take him to. At that time, however, I wasn't as seasoned and mature as I am now so I didn't quite get it. I thought it was just about private schools versus public schools. Needless to say, I picked a school and before long my son was cussing in the middle of the playground, using words we don't use at home, and picking up all kinds of bad habits.

At that point I knew I had to readdress my son's schooling. As I redirected my steps, turned back to the Lord, and said, "Lord, lead me to the right school," He led me to the school my kids are currently attending. I realized it wasn't about whether it was a private or public school, nor was it about being a Christian school, it was about how the school was being run—the principles and values they *practiced* and upheld. When I prayed about it and took the time to assess each school, I found one with a believing principal who not only believed in prayer—and would pray over the kids in her care—but also shared the same Christian values our family does!

God led me to take my son to a school whose curriculum and environment aligned more with my principles and my belief. Just seek and then trust God for guidance, because most times the quality of the school depends on the leaders. Being one type of school or another doesn't automatically qualify or disqualify it. I turned out well not because of the type of school I attended but because I had very good leaders. An example of this is when I was a school newspaper editor, my newspaper teacher taught me a lot about writing, but more than that, she taught me about work ethics and leadership. She used to tell us, "Make sure you're going above and beyond in whatever you do." I heard those words every day for four or five years. "Don't do the bare minimum," is a principle she instilled in those she taught, and it drove us to want to raise the bar on everything we tackled.

Start from Where You Are

The first step to taking control of your child's spiritual, physical, and mental safety is being aware of the possible channels used to convey harmful or dangerous messages. Once you are aware of how and where your child may be negatively influenced, the next step is to make the changes necessary to protect your child. If it's the school your child attends, as was the case with my son, you don't have to accept the school your child has been zoned into. It may seem petty, extremist, or even fanatical, but if you believe that school will be detrimental to your child then do whatever you must to put them into a school with which you are comfortable. It may seem daunting at first, but don't be discouraged by the task ahead of you. Ask for the Holy Spirit's guidance and strength in every decision and action you take, then start from where you are currently, and you will make an enormous difference in the life of your child. Believe me, you will see the dividends in a few short years.

In the privacy of your home you can start by having the conversation with your own children. Draw their attention to what's out there—what to pursue and what to avoid—and above all, teach them the Word of God, and how to pray. Children are never too young to have an age-relevant conversation about their safety and future.

Prayer is your greatest defense and your ultimate form of offense.

Prayer is your greatest defense and your ultimate form of offense, so pray in the Spirit for your family and community. Ask the Holy Spirit for guidance as to what to pray for, and speak to other mothers about praying for their children and their friend's families. Make mothers around you aware of the dire threats facing their families, and of course, I'd recommend sharing this book to get them on board with starting the transformation in your community. You can even start a prayer group for mothers and be specific about your prayers. I have founded two prayer groups focused on praying strategically and tactically for *all* children, while specifically focusing on supporting and empowering mothers with children facing health challenges.

You're coming from a perspective of godly knowledge and understanding, so be prepared to coach and mentor younger mothers, and even volunteer to teach children's church. As an example of the value you can add, I serve in children's church and no matter the age group of the class, each child I carry, or whose hand I hold, I constantly pray for them and their family under my breath. I pray specifically against sickness or disabilities, deflecting arrows I'm well aware are targeted at this generation. Others in the church see me and think I'm just helping with children's church but over every child I carry, I speak a word of blessing. These are kids who I would probably never reach in my own house, but if I'm in a room of eight to ten kids, that's potentially eight to ten families, or generations, that I'm influencing with my prayers, Sunday after Sunday.

Be prepared to use the platforms God has given you but obviously use wisdom, and be respectful of your environment, especially at work. Ministering in a setting where it's not allowed is *not* being godly; it's disruptive and is a bad reflection on your message. If anything, commit to dedicated prayers for your company—the Holy Spirit will provide a strategy you can follow, and open doors for you to share.

Something else I discovered which will assist believers desiring to make a difference at work is an organization called *Faith and Work Movement*[15]. It exists "to equip those in the marketplace to fulfill their purposes and do good, helping to connect, and encourage, those in the marketplace." You will need to go through your Human Resources department, but think of the influence you could have in your workplace if you ask God to make a way, and then work in obedience to His voice.

As mothers, we will have access to different opportunities and platforms depending on where we fit into the society around us. For example, if your husband is a pastor you have a platform to step in and do something. You have a podium and you have access to a microphone—it's a game changer for you. You could even create a department within the church to focus on these matters. Not everyone has access to a podium but depending on where you are, and your level of influence, you can start to effect change. My own life serves as another example—providing this book is my quota to the plan. I'm a career woman with my own business so I have the means to do this. I do not have the pulpit or the podium yet but I'm giving this book. When I serve in the children's church, at a more granular level, I'm offering prayer.

Look for opportunities to transform the world around you to conform to the will of God.

No matter where you are or what your level of influence, as a New Creation Mother you need to be aware of what's going on in the lives of your family, make the changes required to keep them safe from the enemy, and look for opportunities to transform the world around you to conform to the will of God.

TWO HAVE BECOME ONE

When God created man and woman He planned for marriage to represent the union that would later come between Christ and the Church. This revelation is one of the most profound mysteries in the Word of God. In this chapter I will cover what such a godly union means, the power it contains, and how it can be achieved in a marriage between a believing man and a believing woman who strive to live according to the will of God in their individual lives, their marriage, and their family.

First, let's consider what God said after He created Eve: "Therefore a man shall leave his father and mother

God planned for marriage to represent the union that would later come between Christ and the Church.

and be joined to his wife, and they shall become one flesh" (Genesis 2:24). What this means is that a married couple is seen by God as a single unit, or "one flesh." This is not to say these two unique people lose their individuality, but rather to highlight the fact that what God has put together, no man can break apart. Take note of how Jesus responded when tested by the Pharisees, who asked Him, "Is it lawful for a man to divorce his wife for *just* any reason?" (Matthew 19:3):

> [4] And He answered and said to them, "Have you not read that He who made *them* at the beginning 'made them male and female,' [5] and said, 'For this reason a man shall leave his father and mother and be joined to his wife, and the two shall become one flesh'? [6] So then, they are no longer two but one flesh. Therefore what God has joined together, let not man separate."
> Matthew 19:4-6

This statement, given by the One who created Heaven and Earth (Colossians 1:16), points back to God's original plan for a man and woman to be joined together in marriage.

Adam was originally given the task of providing for his family while Eve would bear the children because pregnancy and childbirth are taxing on a woman's body, and having the man provide food, shelter, and protection during this period gives the family a greater chance of survival. You might say, "Well, that worked for ancient cultures, but these days, men and women have an equal footing in life, and it's sexist to assume we should still fit into these traditional roles."

Now this is where a gap in our understanding of biblical principles has caused great division in our modern world. Men and women have *always* had an equal footing in God's Kingdom! Two scriptures make this very clear. Firstly, "God created man in His *own* image; in the image of God He created him; *male and female He created them*" (Genesis 1:27—emphasis mine). Both men and women are created in God's image, so neither is inferior or superior to the other. Secondly, when God created Eve He created a helper who was "comparable" to Adam: "And the Lord God said, '*It is* not good that man should be alone; I will make him a helper comparable to him'" (Genesis 2:18).

Consider a few synonyms for the word "comparable": alike, analogous, correspondent, corresponding, matching, parallel, resembling[16]; and from a second dictionary: equal, equivalent, as good as, in a class with, on a par with, a match for[17]. Given these parallel characteristics there can be no denying men and women were created equal in God's sight. The fact they were given different roles to play within the family structure was to increase stability within the family unit, with the ultimate goal to be that of producing godly children (Malachi 2:15).

The original ideals of first-wave feminism were admirable and some of them still have value, but most aspects of third and fourth-wave feminism have played a role in dividing men and women in various ways, with detrimental consequences as far as raising children within the family. First-wave feminism occurred during the late nineteenth and early twentieth centuries in the Western world. This initial wave focused on legal issues, primarily on securing women's right to vote, and it emerged out of an environment of urban industrialism and liberal, socialist, politics. This was a good and necessary fight despite its liberal, socialist origins, as it reinstated women as equals among men in the eyes of humanity—a fact that has always been true and accepted within God's kingdom. The following three waves of feminism became problematic as they ultimately gave rise to the destruction of the family home and worse. This happened largely through abortion and home instability, given that both parents were now working, and it also drastically propelled the gay liberation movement.

I won't go into further detail about the feminist movement as this is not the platform for it. What I will say is that after securing the right to vote for women, it was helpful in establishing work and pay equality *but feminism does not work in a godly marriage.* Militant attitudes have no place in marriage because God set up the perfect union in harmony, serving one another, sacrificing for one another. Our aim as believers should be to reestablish the original marriage covenant set out by God. I also want to point that I will never use the word "feminist" to describe myself. Rather, I refer to myself using the term my High Priest Jesus calls me—a New Creation! Praise God.

God's definition of marriage provided in the book of Ephesians has distinct roles expected of men and women, implemented to protect the family unit.

[22] Wives, be *subject* to your own husbands, as [a

service] to the Lord. [23] For the husband is head of the wife, as Christ is head of the church, Himself *being* the Savior of the body. [24] But as the church is subject to Christ, so also wives should be subject to their husbands in everything [respecting both their position as protector and their responsibility to God as head of the house]. Ephesians 5:22-24 (AMP)

Both the New and the Old Testaments convey the same message regarding a husband's spiritual authority within a home. This order is patterned after the hierarchy found in Heaven: "But I want you to know that the head of every man is Christ, the head of woman *is* man, and the head of Christ *is* God" (1 Corinthians 11:3).

While some people recoil at the first part of the passage from Ephesians 5 quoted above, concerning wives submitting to their husbands, the verses following this passage put that statement into context:

[25] Husbands, love your wives [seek the highest good for her and surround her with a caring, unselfish love], just as Christ also loved the church and gave Himself up for her, [26] so that He might sanctify the church, having cleansed her by the washing of water with the word [of God], [27] so that [in turn] He might present the church to Himself in glorious splendor, without spot or wrinkle or any such thing; but that she would be holy [set apart for God] and blameless. [28] Even so husbands should *and* are morally obligated to love their own wives as [being in a sense] their own bodies. He who loves his own wife loves himself. [29] For no one ever hated his own body, but [instead] he nourishes *and* protects and cherishes it, just as Christ does the church, [30] because we are members

(parts) of His body. [31] FOR THIS REASON A MAN SHALL LEAVE HIS FATHER AND HIS MOTHER AND SHALL BE JOINED [and be faithfully devoted] TO HIS WIFE, AND THE TWO SHALL BECOME ONE FLESH. [32] This mystery [of two becoming one] is great; but I am speaking with reference to [the relationship of] Christ and the church. [33] However, each man among you [without exception] is to love his wife as his very own self [with behavior worthy of respect and esteem, always seeking the best for her with an attitude of lovingkindness], and the wife [must see to it] that she respects *and* delights in her husband [that she notices him and prefers him and treats him with loving concern, treasuring him, honoring him, and holding him dear]. Ephesians 5:25-33 (AMP)

While God's Word makes it clear that men and women are equal partners, it also stipulates that spiritual leadership in the family home is a role the husband must assume. A husband must love and cherish his wife as he does his own life, and a wife must respect her husband. These biblical principles are not influenced by who earns the bulk, or all, of the household income.

Equal Contribution

Even though traditional roles may have changed in modern times, if these essential biblical principles are ignored, problems will arise in the relationship. For example, if a woman is an equal financial partner in her home, there is certainly a different household dynamic at play. Many men are happy for their wives to go out into the world to hustle like a man and bring money home, but then still expect their wives to prepare and serve dinner to the family after a long day at the office. If both the husband and wife work, the household must be run by both equally, if the wife is contributing equal time to earning a salary. Although submitting to her husband's spiritual authority the wife should have an equal say in how the family budget is applied because her contribution is equal, whether she works outside the home or keeps the home running and dedicates her time to raising the children. If the wife shares the financial load it is reasonable for the husband to participate in the proportionate daily chores of maintaining the home.

Of course, it would be great if we could get back to the days where families thrived on a single income, but that is an entire book in itself. To briefly touch on the reality of today's world, however, in these post-industrial revolution times, it is much more difficult for a family to survive on one income, and as a result many women need to work outside the home (they have no choice due to their circumstance), while some women have the luxury of choosing to work outside the home. It is good to remember,

Men and women are on equal footing in a marriage and their roles are complementary.

though, that a woman who chooses to be a stay-at-home mom, fulfilling the vital function of running the home and taking care of the kids, is no less an equal partner in the home. Men and women are on equal footing in a marriage and their roles are complementary. In other words, you don't both have to earn money, and neither do you both have to change diapers and feed the children every day.

These activities must be discussed and agreed upon for the marriage to functions at its best. Scripture *does* say if a man does not provide for his family, he is worse than a heathen (1 Timothy 5:8), so there is scriptural basis directing men to work and provide. This does not mean a husband cannot and should not help with household duties where possible but if the husband is working ten hours a day and the wife is running the home, it isn't fair if he arrives home and is told it's his turn to do the dishes. Likewise, if he has the day off work and his wife is overwhelmed with the children, he should not demand she make lunch as well (and he can help with the children).

If you're a Christian man who's married to a believing woman, she is first your sister in Christ.

Working together, each partner should do what they can to bless and advance their family, and should definitely avoiding scorekeeping. Scorekeeping is highly detrimental to a marriage, causing you to succumb to the temptation of thinking, *I've done more than you today so you must do something for me.* Aside from the selfish attitude, cognitive bias will *always* skew your opinion to what you have done, and under-assess what your spouse has done.

We need to understand that marriage has an aspect of servant leadership to it—the better you are at serving your family, the better you will lead. No one can demand respect; respect is earned. We're all spiritual beings created in the image of God. Men and women are respective aspects of God—different facets of Him that have been created in His likeness. We're both aspects of God poured into different containers. The idea of gender is only applicable to life on this Earth. This means if you're a Christian man who's married to a believing woman, she is first your sister in Christ. She too is a vital member of this Body of Christ you belong to.

A husband and wife becoming "one flesh" (Genesis 2:24) is physically symbolic of our spiritual union with Christ: "But he who is joined to the Lord is one spirit *with Him*" (1 Corinthians 6:17). Just as man cannot separate a physically married couple who has become one flesh, we cannot be separated from Christ once we are born again (Romans 8:38-39). This demonstrates a consistency in that message of oneness. When we are born again, we are from that point forward *in Christ*—we can't be separated from Him and Christ cannot be separated from us.

The Christian marriage is extremely powerful; two people—a man and a woman—become joined as *believers* in a blood covenant with the monumental power originally intended by God. Because they have accepted Christ and become new creations, they are two separate vessels joined together in carrying the essence of God, and I believe they compound His power if they walk in the Spirit. Just as with the Church, Christ is the head of the marriage relationship, and *He* is the example to be followed.

Christ is the head of the marriage relationship, and He is the example to be followed.

So now that we understand the spiritual significance

of a man and a woman becoming one flesh—a physical type of the spiritual union of Christ and His Church—what is the biblical method to walking in that union?

WORKING IT ALL OUT PRACTICALLY

S ince this book is written primarily for mothers, let us first take a look at what the prime example of a wife and mother in a marriage covenant would be, according to scripture. In the book of Proverbs we find a description of a virtuous, or godly, wife (Proverbs 31:10-31). She fears the Lord and is praised for her wisdom, strength, kindness, work ethic, and entrepreneurial spirit, among other admirable characteristics. Her husband safely trusts her and her worth is put far above rubies.

The Proverbs 31 woman is clearly an Old Testament type or foreshadow of a woman empowered by the Holy Spirit in the New Testament (remember, the Old Testament is the New Testament concealed, and the New Testament is the Old Testament revealed). Although there were many virtuous, godly, influential women under the Old Covenant, and it is certainly true they were empowered by the Holy Spirit, they longed to see our day (Matthew 13:17). This is because we have the superpower that rested on them temporarily—the Holy Spirit—living within us *permanently.* Rightly does Paul marvel that we "have this treasure in earthen vessels" (2 Corinthians 4:7, BLB).

Through the power of the Holy Spirit the New Creation Mother is able to do things she would not be able to do in her natural strength. The core value of the New Creation

The New Creation Mother . . . has been raised up and made to sit in the heavenly places in Christ Jesus.

Mother goes beyond good attributes and character traits. What makes the New Creation Mother so special is the fact she is made alive together with Christ, and has been raised up and made to sit in the heavenly places in Christ Jesus (Ephesians 2:5-6). Those who wish to see her have to look at Christ! She resembles Christ now; she is an heir of God and a joint heir with Christ, according to Romans 8:17.

While the values presented by the Proverbs 31 woman epitomize spiritual success, a New Creation Mother's power to achieve that comes from her ability to access the Holy Spirit. For a young Christian mother who desires to live for Christ, the example of the Proverbs 31 woman is a practical vision to which you can set your horizon, but her relationship with the Holy Spirit will bring the specific, unique revelation regarding her individual calling. Much like Jesus is the Author (Originator) and Finisher (Perfecter) of our faith (Hebrews 12:2), the Proverbs 31 woman presents us with the original image, foreshadowing the strength, beauty, and power of the New Creation Mother, who is pruned and perfected through the Holy Spirit.

Husbands Love Your Wives

In the previous chapter we discussed Ephesians 5 where it says, "Husbands, love your wives, just as Christ loved the church" (Ephesians 5:25a). This means a husband should see his believing wife from the perspective that God sees her—in Christ. Sadly, some men take their wives for granted, neglecting to love and cherish them. These Christian mothers may work outside the home, take care of the children, participate in some form of ministry, evangelize, and still manage to run a decent home. One of the most important needs of a woman is to be appreciated and validated for her efforts and achievements. The strength and beauty of a godly woman is a great and special treasure to her family and brings extraordinary value to her husband, her family, and ultimately to God's Kingdom.

Some men must also realize that mothers have a vital leadership role to play in the family. As much as feminism is poisonous to a family, equally poisonous is the idea that the husband should be the only one who makes decisions for the family. A mother usually has deep insight into the emotional life of her children, for example. Excluding the mother from some decisions impacting the children—as another example—would be unwise. The deeper truth, however, is that we cannot live a godly life without the direction of the Holy Spirit, so ask the Holy Spirit for guidance on how best to lead your family in supporting your wife. A godly woman is a tremendous asset to her home, and when a husband validates and encourages his believing wife to assist in making godly decisions, the spiritual strength and wisdom within the family is raised exponentially.

Husbands, think back to when you were looking for a wife, what sort of woman did you have in mind? Proverbs 31:10 begins by asking the question: "Who can find a virtuous wife." This raises a second question: "What kind of man qualifies to receive a virtuous wife?"

When a husband validates and encourages his believing wife . . . the spiritual strength and wisdom within the family is raised exponentially.

Much depends on a man's spiritual standing with God in relation to the bride he attracts, and similarly, much depends on a father's spiritual standing with God in relation to the safety, security, and sufficiency he provides for his family. Ask any young man to describe his ideal wife; what attributes will she have? No man will say he wants a sloppy, lazy wife who neglects the well-being of the home, and neglects to take care of herself. Most men want a beautiful woman who is not lazy, and will work hard at making their house a home, keeping it clean, ensuring the children are taken care of, and making sure things run smoothly. Essentially, men are looking for a perfect woman to be their wife; a queen alongside them.

This is to be expected, but *are you a king deserving*

of such a queen? There is no chance you will attract a godly queen if you're not behaving like a king. My advice to single men seeking a wife is to choose from among those who serve the Lord, because it is from among these women that future generations of New Creation Mothers will spring. You need to appreciate her

Are you a king deserving of such a queen?

as a daughter of the Most High God, and measure your potential mate by your own spiritual success.

If you are already married, and your wife is faithfully serving the Lord, epitomizing the Proverbs 31 woman, she already has the attributes of a queen in your home: she's in right standing with God, she's a child of God, a king and a priest. She is who you need at your side, so cherish her and shower her with love and appreciation.

For a man to find such a woman he must fit a similar godly mold so he can recognize and appreciate the characteristics inherent in the New Creation Mother. All the rubies in the world can't match a virtuous and capable wife, who is unquestionably more precious to the overall wellbeing of a man than worldly riches.

The message I would like to leave with fathers who have believing wives is you must first recognize and appreciate *who* you have—you have a woman *in Christ*. Learn to treat her accordingly. Once you have recognized who you have, you can start fulfilling your role by loving your wife just as meticulously as you love and care for yourself. Husbands and fathers: support your wives so your children will be raised knowing the godly pattern for life given to us through marriage.

Wives Respect Your Husbands

Just as a man should ensure he is behaving like a king if he expects his wife to be a queen, so should the wife behave like a queen if she expects a king. This is true for the unmarried woman seeking a husband as well. So what are the practical steps a New Creation Mother can take to ensure she is aligned with God's Word in her personal life, in her marriage, and in the way she raises her children? My goal in writing this book is not to be prescriptive about how you live—frankly, it's not my place. My suggestion is for you to learn how to be led by the Holy Spirit. He can best show you how to respond to your individual husband in the way he needs, and how to best serve God in your life. All those questions you have concerning how you can best serve God and keep yourself and your family aligned with His Word should be asked of the Holy Spirit.

For practical guidance in your daily life—should you watch that TV series, or is a glass of wine now and then permissible? Ask the Holy Spirit. The Holy Spirit knows you better than anyone, including yourself, and He will help you to avoid hindrances in your walk with God and in your marriage. Remember though, that while you can take the Holy Spirit's guidance as gospel, always interpret your understanding of His voice in line with the Word of God (the Bible) to be sure you have heard Him correctly. Remember too that the Holy Spirit's counsel for one might not be the same for all: in many cases the Holy Spirit told *you* what is best for *your* life—we can't simply apply this advice to everyone else.

Equally, when we start seeing our husbands from God's perspective, we have the opportunity to walk together in the fullness of God's love. In my own marriage I struggled with many issues until the Holy Spirit started coaching me about how to relate to my husband differently, which began when I started seeing him through the eyes of Christ. Once I started seeing him as Jesus does, I no longer focused on what he was doing and what he wasn't doing. I am honestly not concerned with that anymore. Of course, there are times when the enemy will try to pull this old card, but I have learned to quickly shut it down. I have to battle it in my mind, shut it down and drown it! Even when something seems obvious, I have learned not to prejudge him or the situation that seems troubling.

This is *my* story though, so other women shouldn't take it as gospel for their life. I was given explicit information and instruction from the Holy Spirit about how I should relate to my husband. You need to get your own clear information because the Holy Spirit knows your husband much better than you do. He knows the true intentions of your husband's heart. For unmarried women, when a man acts like he's fallen in love with you, the Holy Spirit will know when he's fraudulent. The same goes the other way; at times it may seem as though a man doesn't care but the Holy Spirit knows how deeply he cares for you, so He guides your behavior to prevent you from blowing things out of proportion. The Holy Spirit is our Comforter and Protector, making sure we don't discard something that is truly good for us.

The truth is, on many occasions our relationship issues are based on what we've seen on television, social media, or what we have heard other people talking about. If we dwell on these outside influences, the stories they tell become doctrines in our mind, wreaking havoc with our thoughts. We end up thinking about them all day, and sometimes even make things up in our own minds, causing us to feel convinced our spouse is doing all these terrible things that often don't even exist. It all comes back to the information we focus on. If you're *not* focusing on God's Word and what the Holy Spirit says to you, it means you're focusing on what the world tells you, creating a stronghold of negative thoughts in your mind. Don't be battle-ready for the next negative event in your relationship, thinking, *I have to be smart; I have to know what he's up to, I have to do this or that just in case...* Why plan for an evil day in your marriage? Always consider the source of your information. Whose Word—or whose words—are you focused on?

An example of how these negative thoughts come upon us suddenly is well expressed in the following scenario: you could be talking to a friend on the phone, and you mention your husband will be coming home late tonight, to which she replies, "Oh, does that happen often?"

"Sometimes," you reply.

"I would check into that," your friend says, with a note of drama and suspicion in her voice.

These are the conversations that cause you to start doubting your partner. Don't allow these thoughts into your mind. Cut them off immediately and start praying for your friend. You know your husband is a good man, so you see him through those eyes. You know he's a hard worker, so if he's coming home late, and you see him through godly eyes, you can simply trust he's working. Weigh up where you received your information, and be sure you are focused on God's Word and what the Holy

Spirit has to say about your life and relationships. Don't be influenced by other people's bad experiences. They don't need to be yours.

I think where many women become derailed and fall into trouble is the day they adopt a self-aggrandized mindset: "I can do better by myself. I'm an independent woman…" You are *not* wiser than God. God knows you are fully capable by yourself. He created you. There is no deficiency in you—He created you with the ability to be self-sufficient, *and yet He also said marriage is good.* I encourage you to focus on God's Word,

Don't be influenced by other people's bad experiences. They don't need to be yours.

and to ask the Holy Spirit for His guidance in all your decision-making processes. If you want to be single, then live for God within the context of your chosen life as a single person. If you decide you *do* want to be married then live for God within the context of your intentional, calculated decision. Where people fall short is when they decide they want to be married but are still operating as a single person. This is unsustainable, and a sure recipe for disaster. Don't agree to become one flesh if you plan to keep living two separate lives—both parties must be in agreement regarding the achievement of their family goals within a godly home.

Allow me to qualify these statements. Becoming one flesh through marriage means agreeing to display outwardly an internal agreement. Essentially, you're projecting a united front spiritually and physically, while both parties still retain their unique, God-given dignity and personal independence. Consider how the Proverbs 31 woman blessed her husband and her household with her thrift, shrewd business acumen, and lovingkindness, while retaining her individual identity as a child of God.

She *chose* to rise early to prepare for the day, calculated her own business risks, and had autonomy regarding how she managed her time and her home. Everything she did was in service to God and her family. She happily accepted being subject to her husband's spiritual authority, yet gracefully exerted her own authority as an Israelite and as a daughter of the Most High. In a similar fashion, her husband had complete trust in her, and her ability to manage their home in excellence, recognizing she was more precious to him than rubies could ever be.

Consider how the Proverbs 31 woman blessed her husband and her household . . . while retaining her individual identity as a child of God.

This is a prime example of two independent children of God working in harmony for God's glory, and to generate and protect the health, safety, and comfort of their family. No chauvinism, no feminism, just one flesh under God! Godly marriages are intended to model heavenly relationships on Earth, indeed even as we saw in chapter 7 in the Ephesians 5 passage where Christ models His love for the Church, and the Church her love for Him. In conclusion, marriages should be a safe haven and the most conducive environment to raise powerful, godly seeds.

A CALL TO SALVATION OR REDEDICATION

If you've read the book to this point, your heart has likely begun to burn with the ideas that have been explained. Right now, I know you'd like to understand in practical terms what it means to be saved by grace, and to receive Jesus into your heart as your personal Savior and Lord. If you have been moved by this message but you are not sure where to start you need not worry... this chapter is for you.

Before we go into this, however, it is important to first clarify: all the ideas in this book—explaining and illuminating the gospel of Jesus Christ—have been imbued with the very life of God, and as such, derive their potency directly from the Word of God (Romans 1:16). The implication here is that because the teachings in this book are based on the Word of God, they go beyond self-help. Furthermore, they will only benefit you in their fullest measure when you take the fundamental step of guaranteeing your eternal destiny in Christ.

"Why do I need to be saved?" might be the next logical question. The answer is simple and not far-fetched. Romans 3:23 says "for all have sinned and fall short of the glory of God." This verse shows that mankind's primary problem is sin. Mankind's sin began when Adam—the first man—sinned against God and fell from the position of honor; a position to which God's glory had elevated him. Ever since, man has been born into, and for the most part lived in, bondage and corruption. This singular event condemned Adam and all his descendants (you and I) to eternal damnation, which is permanent separation from God. This is clearly expressed in Romans 6:23, "For the wages of sin *is* death, but the gift of God *is* eternal life in Christ Jesus our Lord."

Man's inability to save himself necessitated the requirement of his redemption from sin, deliverance from its power, and a further initiation into God's kingdom. This can only happen when man receives the gift of eternal life through spiritual rebirth, given to the world through Jesus. Romans 3:24-26 explains it simply:

> [24] being justified freely by His grace through the redemption that is in Christ Jesus, [25] whom God set forth *as* a propitiation by His blood, through faith, to demonstrate His righteousness, because in His forbearance God had passed over the sins that were previously committed, [26] to demonstrate at the present time His righteousness, that He might be just and the justifier of the one who has faith in Jesus.

This is an eternal love story. Jesus is the sinless sacrificial Lamb of God. He came as an expression of God's undying love for you; so much so that God willingly gave Him to be slaughtered as the sacrificial lamb and atonement for our sins. Not just that, He was tortured and died in your place, and yes, this is why we can boldly say that "Jesus is the only way to God." There is no other way to be restored to God. Jesus is the only official, "God-approved" solution to sin.

Jesus is absolutely worthy of all praise, honor, worship, and adoration for what He accomplished for *you*. He died, poured out His blood in presentation before God's mercy seat, and God, being satisfied the penalty of your sin was paid in full, granted Jesus the power to give you eternal life.

How to Receive the Gift of Eternal Life

In the following three short steps, you will be shown how you can receive God's gift of eternal life and be saved. The basis of these steps is clearly outlined in Romans 10:8-10.

> (A) ACCEPT—You need to accept the sacrifice Jesus made through His death on the cross as atonement

for your sins, since this is the means by which you will be reconciled to God. John 3:16 says, "For God so loved the world that He gave His only begotten Son, that whoever believes in Him should not perish but have everlasting life."

(B)   BELIEVE—Beyond accepting the truth of the sacrificial death of Jesus on the cross, you must also believe in your heart that God raised Him from the dead, back to life, and that He is now glorified in majesty in Heaven as your Lord and Savior. Your faith in the death, burial, resurrection, and glorification of Jesus is key to receiving the gift of salvation. Romans 5:1 says, "Therefore, having been justified by faith, we have peace with God through our Lord Jesus Christ."

(C)   CONFESS—At this juncture, after accepting the truth of His death as atonement for you, and then believing that God raised Him from the dead, you must give expression to this belief not just in your heart, but with your mouth—by confessing (saying it out loud, declaring) Jesus as your Lord and personal savior. This is summarized in Romans 10:8-10:

8 But what does it say? "The word is near you, in your mouth and in your heart" (that is, the word of faith which we preach): 9 that if you confess with your mouth the Lord Jesus and believe in your heart that God has raised Him from the dead, you will be saved. 10 For with the heart one believes unto righteousness, and with the mouth confession is made unto salvation.

Confession here is not the confession of sin, but rather it

is the Greek word *homologeó*[18] which means: to say the same thing or be in agreement with what God has said. It is the affirmation of the Lordship of Jesus over your life.

The question is "Will you accept this astounding gift of salvation today?" I pray you act on the Holy Spirit's gentle word to your heart as He speaks right now. You can be saved from eternal destruction, and you can fulfil your God-given, unique, and very special destiny. All you need to do is turn away from your rebellion against your loving God, confess your violations of His way (your sin), ask Him to re-create your spirit (the real you) in the image of Jesus Christ, and you will be born again. God is waiting on the edge of His throne to accept you.

Please make Jesus Christ the Lord of your life right now by saying these words of prayer, and by fully believing them in your heart you will be saved:

"Oh Lord God, I come to you in the name of Jesus Christ. Your Word says that whosoever shall call upon the name of the Lord shall be saved. I believe in Jesus Christ, the Son of the living God. I believe Jesus died for me and that He was buried, and He was raised from the dead. Right now, I confess with my mouth that Jesus Christ is the Lord of my life. I receive by faith eternal life into my spirit. Thank you Lord for saving my soul. I now have Christ dwelling in me. I am saved, I am born again, I am a new creation. Hallelujah!"

Praise God! If you said this prayer, congratulations! You have now been born again. Welcome to God's family! You belong to God, your loving Father in Heaven. You will spend eternity with Him, and with all your fellow saints in His glory. Hallelujah! Have complete confidence that all your past sins are washed away—you are a completely new creature as 2 Corinthians 5:17 tells us clearly, "Therefore, if anyone *is* in Christ, *he is* a new creation; old things have passed away; behold, all things have become new." Yes, it really is that simple.

1 Peter 2:9 tells us you belong to God and you are nothing less than His royal heir: "But you *are* a chosen generation, a royal priesthood, a holy nation, His own special people, that you may proclaim the praises of Him who called you out of darkness into His marvelous light."

Today you made the most important decision of your life. To follow it through, I encourage you to find a Bible-believing church in your area (meaning they believe in the infallible Word of God and the gifts of the Holy Spirit). To continue your spiritual growth, I would like to recommend the book *Now That You're Born Again* by Chris Oyakhilome, the e-book of which can be downloaded at the following link: https://www.affirmation-train.org/wp-content/uploads/2018/11/01-Now-That-Your-Born-Again.pdf. This will help you start your new life in Christ Jesus. I know it will bless and direct your life according to the principles of God's Word.

Continue on in God's grace, and grow from strength to strength. Please do leave a comment on my social media pages if you received God's wonderful salvation today!

For The Lukewarm

Now if you have already made Jesus your Lord, and have been born again, but you feel like you've become complacent, don't worry, God has not forgotten about you, nor turned His back on you. This is because His gifts and callings are irrevocable (Romans 11:29), and nothing can separate you from His great love (Romans 8:38-39).

Remember, you are the righteousness of God and He does not condemn you. I recommend reading Mark 4:7-19 very closely. It is very insightful and will help you to understand how you got here and what it takes to recommit to your faith life. This passage is known as the Parable of the Sower and explains how the Word of God is obstructed from bearing fruit in some people's lives, yet it does bear fruit in the lives of others.

Verses 18 and 19 are especially pertinent for the lukewarm in Christ, "[18] Now these are the ones sown among thorns; *they are* the ones who hear the word, [19] and the cares of this world, the deceitfulness of riches, and the desires for other things entering in choke the word, and it becomes unfruitful." The reason the Word of God which you received is not producing results in you is because you are receiving the Word amongst thorns. You are allowing other things—the cares of this world, the deceitfulness of riches, and the lusts of other things—to choke the Word of God in your life.

I bring you good news: *you* can change things. Change starts with you, and Jesus shows us this in Luke 21:34, "But take heed to yourselves, lest your hearts be weighed down with carousing, drunkenness, and cares of this life, and that Day come on you unexpectedly." This means you are in charge of your heart and responsible for keeping your mind stayed on God. The Bible also says in Proverb 4:23, "Keep your heart with all diligence, For out of it *spring* the issues of life." *You* are responsible for turning up the heat so your lukewarm heart is boiling again.

The first step is to make up your mind to walk in the fullness of your born-again life. Next is to identify how you got to this point and separate yourself from those things—habits, lifestyles, people, etc. that make you stumble. Then begin to invest dedicated time into confessing (speaking, declaring, announcing) who you are in Christ by confessing God's Word. This is a very important step as it will not only begin to create a consciousness in you, but also align you with the will of the Father. When we confess God's Word we are acknowledging and agreeing with everything God has said about us. Also, we are laying claim to everything we now have as a result of Jesus' finished work.

It is important you do this every day and often through the day. You can say things like, "I am the righteousness of God in Christ Jesus. As He is so am I in this world. The law of the Spirit of life in Christ Jesus is working in me! Eternal life is made manifest in my being, energizing me from within." Go on and on like this consistently until it becomes your lifestyle. You will find yourself aligning and living out this life that the Word of God talks about with ease and it will be very difficult for the Word to be choked.

As referenced in Chapter 4, Emily Preston's *Confessions for Life* book is a great place to start, as it provides a list of confessions for almost every aspect of a person's life. And finally, of course, go back to church. If you do not already have one, find a Bible-believing church in your area. Continue in the reading and learning of the Word.

Also I am of the opinion that being baptized in the Holy Spirit with the evidence of speaking with other tongues is the most effective way to remain on fire for the Lord. Speaking in tongues can essentially be considered an "encrypted" heavenly language that gives you direct access to God through the utterance of the Holy Spirit within you. In the Bible we find references to both "speaking" and "praying" in tongues, and these terms are often used interchangeably, despite some clear differences. The distinctions of both speaking and praying in tongues are beyond the scope of this book so please email me or engage me on my social media platforms for more information. Just know that spending time in prayer (mostly in tongues) corporately or individually is one of the keys to growing in faith.

Speaking/Praying in Tongues—Your Spiritual Superpower

In chapter two I shared that the Holy Spirit is the *action power* of God. Your call to action is to engage the power of the Holy Spirit, and this is achieved through first receiving the baptism of the Holy Spirit and then praying in the Spirit consistently, using your new heavenly language. In this section I will share with you the power and benefits of speaking in tongues.

Just before Jesus ascended into Heaven He reminded his disciples of an earlier promise He had made, "And I will pray the Father, and He will give you another Helper, that He may abide with you forever" (John 14:16). During this period of time—after His resurrection but before His ascension—Jesus explained to His disciples they did not have much longer to wait before receiving the Helper He had promised:

> [4] And being assembled together with them, He [Jesus] commanded them not to depart from Jerusalem,

but to wait for the Promise of the Father, "which," He said, "you have heard from Me; [5] for John truly baptized with water, but you shall be baptized with the Holy Spirit not many days from now." (Acts 1:4– parentheses mine)

Shortly after Jesus said these words He ascended to be with the Father. The disciples waited for the fulfillment of this promise, and true to His Word, not long after that the Holy Spirit came from Heaven to Earth, making quite the entrance to the gathered disciples, and He filled them in a mighty way with the power of His Spirit!

[1] When the Day of Pentecost had fully come, they were all with one accord in one place. [2] And suddenly there came a sound from heaven, as of a rushing mighty wind, and it filled the whole house where they were sitting. [3] Then there appeared to them divided tongues, as of fire, and one sat upon each of them. [4] And they were all filled with the Holy Spirit and began to speak with other tongues, as the Spirit gave them utterance. (Acts 2:1-4)

Jesus' promise to give us a Helper who will abide with us forever (John 14:16) means all believers, even today, can choose to be filled with the Holy Spirit. One of the advantages of receiving the Holy Spirit is the divine ability to speak and pray in tongues—a heavenly language that your spirit-man and God understand. Praying in tongues is a powerful part of our spiritual walk, so much so that when Paul discovered a group of about twelve disciples in

When you pray in tongues you are planning things the enemy can never access nor manipulate.

Ephesus who hadn't heard about the Holy Spirit, he made sure to lay hands on them so that the Holy Spirit filled them, and they spoke with tongues and prophesied (Acts 19:6).

In 1 Corinthians 14:2 we read, "For he who speaks in a tongue does not speak to men but to God, for no one understands *him*; however, in the spirit he speaks mysteries." The mysteries we speak referred to in this verse is a language the enemy cannot understand nor decode, making it the safest form of prayer. We have discussed that the world has a well-calculated agenda against your family and your children, which makes the need to pray in tongues all the more urgent. Being something like a spiritual code, when you pray in tongues you are planning things the enemy can never access nor manipulate. You are setting up spiritual defensive structures, securing your children and family.

A believer who speaks in a spiritual tongue edifies and improves himself (1 Corinthians 14:4), so praying in tongues will help you progress in your spiritual walk, causing you to rise like an edifice and operate at your highest level of faith (Jude 1:20, AMP). When we speak in tongues, we edify ourselves, we improve ourselves, and we promote ourselves, making this a wonderful "self-building" benefit available to us!

Praying in tongues also provides the perfect undiluted language to express the purest praise and worship to God. Being a language of the Spirit, it is not contaminated or restricted by the limitations of earthly languages, so your prayer, praise, and worship, will be limited if you don't pray in tongues.

When you pray, it is important to first pray in tongues

before praying in your own understanding (1 Corinthians 14:15), because when you pray in your understanding you can only pray what you know and it may not be adequate for the situation. When you speak in tongues, though, there are no limitations because you are speaking spiritual mysteries.

While there is certainly a place in your life for dedicated prayer—and it is good to dedicate time when there are little to no distractions—my favorite thing about praying in tongues is that you can pray in tongues anywhere, at any time, on the go, in bed, in the shower… anywhere! This is because not relying on your own understanding doesn't require the same type of concentration as thinking about what you are praying.

Being the prayer of the New Testament, praying in tongues is the prayer of the *New Creation Mother*. I think

Your prayer, praise, and worship, will be limited if you don't pray in tongues.

God was thinking about mothers when He planned for people to pray in the Spirit. He knew how busy mothers can be, so He provided a prayer we could take anywhere with us *while still effecting a great impact!* Isaiah 28:12 says, "'This is the rest with which You may cause the weary to rest," And, "This is the refreshing.'" Isn't this remarkable? A prayer that doesn't require us to sweat it out, but at the same time produces *mighty results!*

Personally, I strive to pray in tongues for no less than two hours every day. In case you wonder how this is achievable, let me explain. Start your day by dedicating between thirty and sixty minutes to praying in tongues, then throughout your day find ten to fifteen minutes here and there to pray whenever you can. If you know you are going to be busy with chores, doing laundry, or cooking, set your timer and start praying. Praying in tongues brings a sense of peace, and also ensures your spirit is not idle amidst your business.

Learn not to allow long periods of idleness in your day, except when you intentionally want to rest in silence. Rather than allowing your mind to wander, with all manner of thoughts going through your mind, occupy your time praying in tongues. If you learn to set your timer for when you know you will have an opportunity to pray in tongues, you will be amazed at how quickly you can surpass two hours every day.

Being the prayer of the New Testament, praying in tongues is the prayer of the New Creation Mother .

Of course, this does require you being *intentional* about it, but it is certainly doable.

Imagine how quickly the atmosphere in our homes would change if more mothers frequently prayed in tongues! Our children would soon begin to imitate us, developing into giants for the kingdom. Just think of the world we would create; a world filled with heavenly activities where angels are activated daily to work for and minister to us as required in their job description (Hebrews 1:14), but for this to happen we have to actively engage them.

Hallelujah! I believe the Holy Spirit is guiding you to make the right decision today.

My God richly bless you, New Creation Mother! I pray this book touched your heart, and will bless you for years to come. Please reach out to me and let me know what the Lord is doing in your life. Go forth in the boldness and authority of your inheritance as a King and a Priest, and bring the kingdom of your almighty Father down to this Earth and restore it to His will.

Love, Winnie.

Endnotes

1. Mumford, S. D., and E. Kessel. 1986. "Role of Abortion in Control of Global Population Growth." Clinics in Obstetrics and Gynaecology 13, no. 1: 19–31. https://pubmed.ncbi.nlm.nih.gov/3709011/ (accessed September 8, 2021).
2. Kennedy, Jr, Robert. 2021. Campaign to Restore Child Health. Children's Health Defense. https://childrenshealthdefense.org/campaign-restore-child-health/ (accessed 8 September 2021].
3. CDC. 2018. "Data and Statistics on Children's Mental Health." Centers for Disease Control and Prevention. CDC. 2018. https://www.cdc.gov/childrensmental-health/data.html (accessed September 8, 2021).
4. "Https://Twitter.com/Cspan/Status/1364999967635603462." n.d. Twitter. https://twitter.com/cspan/status/1364999967635603462 (accessed September 8, 2021).
5. "G509 - anōthen - Strong's Greek Lexicon (KJV)."
6. G2537 - kainos - Strong's Greek Lexicon (KJV).
7. Ibid (Thayer's Greek Lexicon)
8. Preston, Emily. "Confessions for Life: God's Promises for You PDF | Faith Talks." https://faithtalks.com.au/confessions-for-life-latest-march-20/, (accessed October 25, 2021).
9. McDermott, Deborah M A, and Andrew Wommack. 2019. Autism Healed: One Woman's Fight to Save Her Sons.
10. Reyes, Mara De Los. 2021. Hope for a Healed Child: One Mother's Daring Journey of Faith. Cypress, California: Square Tree Publishing.

11. Osteen, Dodie. 2003. Healed of Cancer. Houston, Texas: Lakewood Church Publication.

12. "Free Resources | Faith Talks." n.d. https://faithtalks.com.au/free-resources/.

13. School, The Healing. n.d. "Enter the Healing School with Pastor Chris." Enterthehealingschool.org. Accessed November 7, 2021. https://www.enterthehealingschool.org/books.php.

14. "Signs & Wonders Camps - Children's Summer Camps IHOPKC." n.d. Signs & Wonders. Accessed November 18, 2021. https://www.ihopkc.org/signsandwonders/

15. "Faith and Work Movement | Home - Silicon Valley and SF Bay Area." https://www.faithandworkmovement.org/ (accessed September 13, 2021).

16. "Thesaurus Results for COMPARABLE." n.d. merriam-Webster.com. Accessed December 23, 2021. https://www.merriam-webster.com/thesaurus/comparable.

17. "Comparable." n.d. TheFreeDictionary.com. Accessed December 23, 2021. https://www.freethesaurus.com/comparable.

18. Strong's Concordance #3670, https://biblehub.com/greek/3670.htm, (accessed January 31, 2022)